Proud to Be:
Writing by
American Warriors
Volume 5

Southeast Missouri State University Press • 2016

Proud to Be:
Writing by
American Warriors
Volume 5

Edited by Susan Swartwout

Partners in the Military-Service Literature Series

Proud to Be: Writing by American Warriors, Volume 5
Copyright by Southeast Missouri State University Press.
All rights reserved. Permission to reprint a particular
author's individual work will be granted upon that
author's request to the University Press.

ISBN: 978-0-9979262-0-0

First Published in the United States of America, 2016
Southeast Missouri State University Press
One University Plaza, MS 2650
Cape Girardeau, MO 63701
http://www.semopress.com

Cover photograph: *Always Time For Chai* by A. Sean Taylor
Cover design: Carrie M. Walker

Southeast Missouri State University Press, founded in 2001, serves
as a first-rate publisher in the region and produces books, *Big Muddy:
Journal of the Mississippi River Valley*, *The Cape Rock* poetry journal, and
the Faulkner Conference series.

The Missouri Humanities Council is a 501(c)3 non-profit organization that was created in 1971 under authorizing legislation from the
U.S. Congress to serve as one of the 56 state and territorial humanities councils that are affiliated with the National Endowment for the
Humanities.

Contents

David Chrisinger

Introduction: Making Sense of the Unknown

The true era of modern warfare began with the American Civil War, where highly destructive weapons, coupled with masses of soldiers available for slaughter, resulted in the first public exhibition of the murderous realities of modern military technology. Between 650,000 and 850,000 Americans died as a result of combat, accidents, starvation, and disease during that horrendous conflict. With such grave losses, President Abraham Lincoln was tasked with making sense of what had happened. After all, if there was no reason for the losses, no meaning for them, how could he expect his constituents to support the fighting, to do what needed to be done to win the war?

"These honored dead shall not have died in vain," he told a crowd of 15,000–20,000 in Gettysburg, Pennsylvania, a few months after the bloodiest battle of the war: "We cannot dedicate—we cannot consecrate—we cannot hallow—this ground. The brave men, living and dead, who struggled here, have consecrated it, far above our poor power to add or detract. The world will little note, nor long remember what we say here, but it can never forget what they did here. It is for us the living, rather, to be dedicated here to the unfinished work which they who fought here have thus far so nobly advanced. It is rather for us to be here dedicated to the great task remaining before us—that from these honored dead we take increased devotion to that cause for which they gave the last full measure of devotion—that we here highly resolve that these dead shall not have died in vain—that this nation, under God, shall have a new birth of freedom—and that government of the people, by the people, for the people, shall not perish from the earth."

"In the address," writes historian Drew Gilpin Faust, "the dead themselves become the agents of political meaning and devotion; they act even in their silence and anonymity. Lincoln immortalized them as the enduring inspiration for an immortal nation." Unlike the "honored dead," the Union would not "perish from the earth." "Soldiers' deaths," Faust continues, "like Christ's sacrifice, became the vehicle of salvation, the means for a terrestrial, political redemption."

For those who believed in the cause—to preserve the Union—the loss of life was not meaningless. Those who lost a loved one in this "noble affair" were able to derive solace from the fact that their loved one had died for a worthy cause—so that a nation might live. "In some ways," writes Holocaust survivor Viktor Frankl, "suffering ceases to be suffering at the moment it finds a meaning."

"But not all Americans were satisfied with such a justification of war's cost," Faust concludes. "The horrors of battle and the magnitude of the carnage were difficult to put aside. The force of loss left even many believers unable to abandon lingering uncertainties about God's benevolence. Doubters confronted profound questions not just about God but about life's meaning and the very foundations of both belief and knowledge."

Louis Menand has argued that the Civil War not only "discredited the beliefs and assumptions of the era that preceded it." In addition, the war destroyed "almost the whole intellectual culture of the North." Oliver Wendell Holmes, Jr, who was wounded at Antietam, was one of the men who Menand said had resolutely rejected the idea that dying in war was a glorious sacrifice. Holmes had volunteered to fight, Menand explains, because of certain moral principles, but "the war did more than make him lose those beliefs. It made him lose his belief in beliefs." This was more than just a loss of faith, writes Faust, "it was an issue of both epistemology and sensibility, of how we know the world and how we envision our relationship to it."

Fifty-two years after the Civil War ended, the United States entered another modern war—the First World War. Unlike the Civil War, however, it was difficult for many to justify America's involvement. Despite President Woodrow Wilson's claim that the war would be fought to "end all wars" and "make the world safe for democracy," American men did not rush to enlist. According to historian Howard Zinn, "A million men were needed, but in the first six weeks after the declaration of war only 73,000 volunteered. Congress voted overwhelmingly for a draft."

The Wilson administration also punished—through the Espionage Act—anyone who refused to get in line. Perhaps the most famous of dissenters, the leader of the American Socialist Party, Eugene Debs, was prosecuted and sentenced to 10 years in prison for strongly opposing American entry into the First World War and for urging young men to resist the draft. During one speech he gave in Canton, Ohio, in June 1918, Debs argued: "They tell us that we live in a great free republic; that our institutions are democratic; that we are a free and self-governing people. That is too much, even for a joke. . . . Wars throughout history have been waged for conquest and plunder. . . . And that is war in a nutshell. The master class has always declared the wars; the subject class has always fought the battles."

Looking back, Debs's argument seems moderate and hardly arguable. Here's how Zinn put it: "In 1914 a serious recession had begun in the United States. J. P. Morgan later testified: 'The war opened during a period of hard times. . . . Business throughout the country was depressed, farm prices were deflated, unemployment was serious, the heavy industries were working far below capacity and bank clearings were off.' But by 1915, war orders for the Allies (mostly England) had stimulated the economy, and by April 1917, more than \$2 billion worth of goods had been sold to the Allies. As Hofstadter says: 'America became bound up with the Allies in a fateful union of war and prosperity.'"

In the end, about 10 million died on the battlefields of the First World War. Another 20 million died of hunger and disease related to the war. As Dr. Edward Tick has pointed out, the First World War was a "massive exercise in technology-driven slaughter wholesale to the point of meaninglessness." The death and suffering finally ended with the unconditional surrender of Germany on November 11, 1918—Armistice Day.

Since that day, no one to my knowledge has ever been able to show that the war brought any positive gain for humanity. "The older I get," said one American veteran of that war decades afterwards, "the sadder I feel about the uselessness of it all." We know now, of course, that the First World War didn't end all wars; instead, it was simply a harbinger of greater death and suffering to come.

So how can we make sense of such a meaningless war? The most visible and emotionally charged way the victors attempted to make meaning of the First World War was through the commemoration of fallen soldiers. Each of the victors—the United States, Great Britain, and France—attempted to glorify the rank and file through national memorials to the Unknown Soldier, who came to represent the masses sent to die and be quickly forgotten. The Unknown Soldier gave a face to those anonymous dead—a face that could be molded to resemble whomever we choose. He also served to glorify their sacrifice.

On Armistice Day 1921, the day America's Unknown Soldier was buried at the National Cemetery in Arlington, Virginia, George Rothwell Brown wrote in *The Washington Post* that the Unknown Soldier was a "well-loved son of the republic" who "sleeps at last shrouded in his immortality." "A hundred millions of people," Brown continues, "have called him 'son,' and given him a name that for all time to come in every heart shall be a synonym for sacrifice and loyalty.

"In honoring him with solemn rite and ritual the mighty country for which he gladly gave his life touched a new and loftier height of majesty and dignity, as though the very government itself took on resplendent luster from the simple nobility of its humble dead."

"Never before," Brown writes, "did the hero have so wonderful a burial, so inspiring in its symbolism. Never had Americans found in such symbolism such depths of spiritual meaning."

"It was," according to historian Omar Bartov, "this identification of the living nation with its anonymous but glorified fallen soldiers provided a means to come to terms with the trauma of war." "The unknown soldier," Bartov continues, "fulfilled the requirement of both focusing on the suffering and sacrifice of the individual, for which a powerful need existed, and of distancing oneself from any particular fallen member of family or community."

Because the Unknown Soldier had been endowed with a higher meaning, he inadvertently legitimized forgetting that war is largely an affair of senseless slaughter. In other words, he helped pave the way for future sacrifice by glorifying the actions of the combatants and enhancing the nobility of the dead. As Bartov argues, "Mourning will, in turn, focus on the service rendered by the dead for the nation's historical mission and future. Rather than being deprived of its sons, the nation is enriched for those who die for it."

By concentrating on individual devotion, suffering, and sacrifice, however, we unwittingly created a chasm between those who "had been there" and those who had not, in which those who had been sent to fight and die often felt abandoned and misunderstood upon their return by the society that had sent them. Because we were not—as a country—honest about the wastefulness and meaninglessness of the First World War, and because we chose instead to revel in the war's meaning and elevate those who were lost to a heroic status, we unwittingly caused rage, resentment, frustration, and disillusionment among the veterans who had learned firsthand that the war had not accomplished much of anything.

Because of advances in battlefield technology and modern science, we will likely never have another "unknown soldier." In what way, then, will we be able to make meaning of the wars in Afghanistan and Iraq? I believe we can make meaning by giving those who witnessed the wastefulness and meaninglessness of these wars a platform to tell us their stories. Instead of pushing a collective meaning based on the glory of sacrifice, we should allow them to tell us what the war meant to them, as individuals. If instead of monuments to the dead, we offered veterans a chance to offer themselves to the public, we as a society could better identify with them. Their truths would not be lost, and their stories would not be adulterated. Instead of idolizing them and the abstract concepts they "willingly" gave their lives for, we could feel connected in a deeply personal and universal way. Only then, I believe, can we truly make sense of the unknown.

David Chrisinger is an Associate Lecturer at the University of Wisconsin–Stevens Point, where he teaches a student-veteran reintegration course. He is also the editor of a collection of essays written by student veterans titled *See Me for Who I Am*. He is the son of a Vietnam-era Army veteran and the grandson of an Army veteran who fought in the Battle of Okinawa during the Second World War.

Winners and Finalists of the
Writing Contest

Essays judged by Dr. Adam Criblez, Director of the Center for Regional History, Southeast Missouri State University

Winner: Jarrod L. Taylor for "Section 60"
From Adam Criblez:

Powerfully emotional. The author transports readers to Arlington National Cemetery, where the narrator, a veteran of recent wars in Iraq, has taken students to visit the monument. Although the students appear just briefly, they are an important foil for the narrator, who wants them to somehow understand the selfless patriotism symbolized by those buried in the hallowed grounds. For the narrator, the visit is not about the changing of the guard at the Tomb of the Unknown Soldier or Robert E. Lee's house. Instead, as the narrator concludes: "This, America, is what sacrifice looks like. This is what I wish my students could see and understand." The writing is raw and emotional, and I appreciated that it was not set on a battlefield, but instead explored how poignant past events and lost friends can remain.

Honorable Mentions: Ken McBride for "The Massillon Boys" and Leonard Adreon for "The Forgotten War: A Personal Reflection on the Korean War"

Photography judged by Fred Lynch, Photographer, *Southeast Missourian* newspaper

Winner: A. Sean Taylor for "Always Time for Chai"
From Fred Lynch:

The winning photo has a raw reality to it. It is a captured moment that I have never seen. After confirming that chai is tea, I realized that the photographer chose to document a friendly encounter between a soldier and a civilian. While the location is not known, the military presence seems welcome. The image reflects peace.

Honorable Mentions: Jarrod L. Taylor for "Innocence Reflected" and Journey Carolyn Collins for "Forgiven Too"

Poetry judged by Terry Lucas, Co-Executive Editor of Trio House Press, and the son of WWII Veteran, SSgt. Americus Millard Lucas. In addition to his poetry collection, *If They Have Ears to Hear*, winner of the 2012 Copperdome Chapbook Award, Terry has two full-length poetry collections: *In This Room* (CW Books, 2016) and *Dharma Rain*, forthcoming from Saint Julian Press.

Winner: Bill Glose for "Questions Raised by Black Scorpions"
From Terry Lucas:

In "Questions Raised by Black Scorpions," the sound work, the imagery, the internal and external conflict, and the questions raised by war were embodied in "these segmented, / scabrous creatures... / ... pincers raised, / tail curled into a venom-spiked question mark." And all aspects of the poem worked in concert to lead to a climax where "Each man / [was] swimming in an ocean of questions" with no answers other than "destinations on maps inscribed with / grease-marker circles." The poet had my ear from the opening half- and slant-rhymes of "knew/ boots" and "thought/but." But those "letters we'd written / 'just in case' burning like coals in our pockets" clinched the deal. Every line of this poem in some way seemed to enact the questions raised by war— questions that remained unanswered through the final line. In the end, the diction, the open-endedness, and the passion of this poem were undeniable.

Honorable Mentions: Bryan Nickerson for "Runaway Slave" and Milton J. Bates for "First Blood"

Fiction judged by Dixon Hearne, author of *Delta Flats: Stories in the Key of Blues and Hope*; *From Tickfaw to Shongaloo*; *Plantatia: High-toned and Lowdown Stories from the South*; and *Plainspeak: New and Collected Poems*.

Winner: Tessa Poppe for "A Bird"
From Dixon Hearne:

"A Bird" is the compelling story of one soldier's struggle to deal with post-war trauma. The writer uses flashback to connect two seemingly unrelated events. When the narrator encounters a bird lying face-up in his yard one morning, chest heaving and growing weak, she feels powerless to help the creature and tries to ignore it. But the weakened bird stirs dark images in her mind of a defenseless Pakistani boy she had watched being raped by a family member behind his squalid one-room house. Because the "rules of engagement" prevented soldiers from interfering in civilian matters, she must bear silent witness to the atrocity. Like the bird, the frail boy could not move—an image the soldier cannot erase from her mind or memory. Through effective use of symbolism, the writer portrays all three of them as victims of circumstance. The images are palpable, the story beautifully told.

Honorable Mentions: Kyle Larkin for "Into Dust" and Jason Arment for "Bottle Rockets and Bad Memories"

Interviews judged by Dr. Susan Kendrick, chairperson of the Department of English. She teaches courses in early modern English literature, including the plays of Shakespeare, whose study of commanders and soldiers in war in "The Life of King Henry V" is one of her favorite plays.

Winner: Caleb Nelson for "90 Minutes: Interview with Ryan Pitts"
From Susan Kendrick:

The "Interview with Ryan Pitts" stood out to me first because of Mr. Pitts' definition of "what defines an American"—"you want to be an American, guess what, today you're an American." His attitude is one of inclusion of all races and creeds in the makeup of American culture. His narrative emphasizes the teamwork necessary in military service, and his recital of the names of his deceased comrades, along with his statement that he lives to do the things that he cannot—that his life has become a memorial to the lives of his friends who made the ultimate sacrifice—is moving and profound. His recollection of the events of the battle and his descriptions of his friends' heroism were immediate and tragic.

Honorable mentions: Casey Titus for "Interview: Preserving a Dying Legacy" and David Chrisinger for "Interview with Major (R) Jonathan Silk"

Award-Winning Writing

Essay Winner

Jarrod L. Taylor

"Section 60"

Our tour bus stopped among other tour buses, and our driver, George, grabbed the microphone.

"Okay, kids," he said. "I know that Arlington is a beautiful place, and while you're here, you may see a funeral. This is an active cemetery. I'm going to ask you for a favor, though. If you see that horse-drawn carriage with a flag-draped casket, don't snap that picture. That's someone's loved one under that flag. It's someone who has served our nation. As a Vietnam vet with buddies in here, I'm asking that you just don't take that picture."

My students rose from their seats and started filing toward the front of the bus and down the steps out into the parking lot. Once everyone was off, we gathered in front of the visitor center to get a count.

We couldn't have asked for better weather for a day of touring the memorials and monuments in and around Washington, D.C. It was a relatively quiet Monday morning, and the sky was a clear and deep infantry blue. It was a little cool, only 52 degrees in May, but the sun was still low in the morning sky. There was a light breeze blowing through the trees that reminded us that summer hadn't arrived yet.

I passed through the visitors' center with my students and the other chaperones, but I had already discussed with the tour guide and other chaperones that I would be splitting from the group once we were inside.

The tour guide headed off toward the Tomb of the Unknown Soldier, and the gaggle of students and parent chaperones followed. As we reached Eisenhower Avenue, I got the other adults' attention and pointed that I was heading left when they were going straight. They nodded, and I started down Eisenhower to visit my friends.

Arlington National Cemetery, I thought as I looked out over the rows of white headstones disappearing over the rolling hills.

Damn, it's been a long time. Too long; hell, last time I was here, Josh and Shawn still had temporary markers. It must have been 12 or 13 years ago. Too damn long.

I walked down Eisenhower Avenue toward Section 60, the final resting place for all of my friends who are buried here. Even part of my great uncle's remains are buried here in a mass grave with the rest of his B-25 crew. They crashed a month before D-Day, but they didn't make it home until 2010. I had the honor of escorting my great uncle's casket back to our hometown.

The students I brought here are tourists. They are here to see the sights: the changing of the guard, the Kennedy gravesites, Robert E. Lee's house. They won't understand. Maybe that's a good thing. Maybe we did our jobs well enough that they won't ever have to get it. I, on the other hand, have had half a dozen or more friends buried here since the last time I visited.

I walked past the different sections, 54, 55, 59 and looked at the stones. *Born 1920, died 1944, and his wife Vera. Born 1926, died 1944...*

As I neared Section 60, I felt the tears coming closer. I was choking back tears, but I wasn't even sure why. I was never particularly close to the friends I have buried here, and I never met my great uncle. I played golf with Jason, helped train Kyle, and I got to know Josh pretty well, but I wasn't really part of his clique.

Come on, Jarrod. Get your shit together. I kept walking.

I stopped and downloaded the Arlington app on my phone. I knew were Kyle was located, and I had an idea about Josh and Shawn, but I wasn't certain. Plus, messing with my phone gave me something else to think of. I won't have to cry if I'm occupied.

Section 60

Here goes, I tell myself. *I'll visit each of the guys, have a good cry, then I'll get back to my students.*

I reached the middle of Section 60 and turned into the grass, walking between the stones. The last time I was here, Josh and Shawn were the last two buried in their row. Section 60 still had a lot of empty space then. Now it's filled.

I found Josh and Shawn, right next to each other. I spent a few moments there, took some photos, and brushed bird shit off of one of the stones. Then I turned to look for Kyle's grave.

My mother and stepfather were here when Kyle was buried. I was in Iraq, but I saw a photo that someone had taken, and I saw my parents there in the back of the crowd. It just so happened that they were on vacation in Virginia when everything happened, so they were able to be there. I was glad. Now, my mom is gone too. I wish I had that picture of them there in the back of the funeral gathering.

I walked through the rows of headstones, looking at the numbers and counting down until I reached Kyle's marker, *Section 60, 8666.*

Just as I spotted Kyle's stone, I saw her: a beautiful young woman in her early twenties, I would say. She wore a blue dress that stopped just above her knees, covered by a tan overcoat that hung open, and nude high heels. Her lips were bright red and her blonde hair hung to her shoulders, blowing in the cool morning breeze.

At first, she seemed out of place to me, as she walked among the stones in my direction.

She walked through the grass, careful not to let her heels sink into the grass, until she found her spot. There was a small shade tree between stones, and I could tell she knew it well. She approached the tree, placed a blanket at its base and sat down.

I did my best not to make eye contact with her. I wanted so badly to talk to her, to ask questions, to tell her that I'm sorry. As I glanced in her direction, I could see the tears on her face, as she sat there twisting her wedding ring around her finger.

I couldn't fight the tears anymore. She was so young, her whole life ahead of her and already a widow. He had probably been just as young, just as much life ahead of him. She reminded me of my own wife when I went off to war for the first time. *What if?* I wondered.

They were probably just starting out, newlyweds, excited to start living once he came home, but he couldn't. She sat there crying softly, talking to him. Later, she moved closer to the stone. Sitting in the grass above her dead husband's body, talking to him as if he were calling from overseas. She told him what she'd been doing and how much she missed him. She shared some gossip from her friends and talked about having dinner with his parents.

So young. Such a tragedy.

I was happy to see beer bottle caps on Kyle's headstone. Sunday had been the anniversary of his death, and other friends had been there recently. I knelt and cried. I apologized, feeling guilty but knowing I couldn't have done anything to change the circumstances.

After spending a few moments, I stood and started to walk away, but then I turned back toward her. I wanted so badly to walk over and say something. I was there for the same reason, to cry and talk to old friends who never came home. In the end, I couldn't. What would I say? Besides, this was her time with her husband.

I stood there, crying for my own friends, and for her, and for her husband, whom I'd never met. *Such a shame*, I thought. I walked one row further and found Jason and Derek, and several other soldiers' names on a stone. They were good guys. I knew what it meant when I saw several names on one stone. It meant that they couldn't figure out who was who after the helicopter accident. Still another row over I found my great uncle's stone, with a few other names on it, the unidentifiable remains buried together.

While I was there, visiting other graves, another young woman approached. She said hello to the girl in blue. Maybe they knew each other. Maybe their husbands had served together, or maybe they had met here, while mourning their men.

They sat in the grass, two stones apart, talking to each other and talking to their husbands.

This, America, is what sacrifice looks like. This is what I wish my students could see and understand.

Jarrod L. Taylor served as an infantryman in the U.S. Army from 2000–2009. During that time, he deployed to Uzbekistan and Afghanistan in 2001–2002, Horn of Africa in 2003, Afghanistan in 2004–2005, and Iraq from 2007–2009. He received a BA in History from Eastern Illinois University in 2013, and he currently resides in Shelbyville, Kentucky, with his wife and two children.

Ken McBride

The Massillon Boys

> *We remember the men who die in battle but sometimes overlook*
> *those who lost their lives in support of these causes from non-*
> *combat related reasons. They deserve the same level of recogni-*
> *tion and respect.*
> *Following is one story out of thousands. . . .*

January 11, 1967.

Wednesday morning. I had just awakened from another night sleeping on the ground under my poncho. I was starting to prepare my daily allotment of 'C' rations when my team leader informed me we would be leaving Operation Sierra, a combat mission in the Vietnam Central Highlands, and returning to our base camp in Chu Lai. I had not had a shower, clean clothes, or regular food for the last 33 days. Caked in mud and soaked from the monsoon rains, I was a willing recipient of this news.

Trained as combat engineers and not as infantry riflemen, the members of my unit, the 1st Shore Party Battalion, often joined line units and fought alongside the 'grunts.' Our duties, as opposed to traditional combat engineering, were to facilitate coordination of supplies and to direct helicopters as they flew in with the goods. This involved standing up in the open to use arm signals to guide the pilots. This was not high on my list of favored activities.

The search and destroy mission of Operation Sierra was not ending but only our involvement in it. When our relief chopper arrived, we were happy to climb onboard and leave the battle behind. I survived the previous month with no significant injury except slicing my thumb with a machete while hacking through the jungle. Approximately half an hour later, we arrived back in Chu Lai. Six members of my company were preparing to board the same helicopter and take our place in the field.

Three of these men were from Ohio, one from Alabama, one from West Virginia and one from Georgia. The men from Ohio were all from the same hometown—Massillon—a small community in the NE corner of the state.

In the mid 1960s there was no draft lottery—no lucky and unlucky numbers; instead, when you turned 18, a letter came from the government telling you to register at the local draft board. You received a small white card with a number / letter code on it. A designation of 1-A meant you were going. Few had the wealth or privilege to avoid this fate. The Massillon boys received these cards, along with other 18 year olds lacking a way out.

With conscription looming, Tim Berry and his two best friends, William Coyne and Richie Fuchs joined the Marine Corps on the buddy plan so they could stay together during training and assignment in Vietnam. I was from Missouri and followed a similar path of enlistment and deployment to Southeast Asia, where I met and became friends and comrades with the men from Ohio.

The men were childhood friends, their homes within a couple of blocks of each other. One grew up Catholic and the other two Protestant. Tim and Richie went to the public elementary school while Bill attended St. Joseph's Parish school. Later they came together at Massillon's Washington High School where legendary football coaches Paul Brown and Earle Bruce spent time before leading Ohio State to football prominence. Tim and Richie graduated in 1964 and Bill in '65.

They grew up on the west side. It was then, as now, a community of close-knit, hardworking people. In the 1960s, it struggled with economic hardship like much of the industrial northeast. Lacking the opportunity for organized sports, they played in the street, backyards, and vacant lots. Sometimes they spent time together at the Massillon Boys and Girls Club. Often meeting at Watts Confectionary, nicknamed Wattzies, the west-siders considered the burgers, fries, and shakes the best in the entire Buckeye state. The proprietor allowed them to read magazines and comic books from his newsstand as long as they were buying things.

The trio had jobs and worked hard to become proud owners of new cars. Richie had a '65 Dodge Coronet; Tim, a '65 Mustang; and Bill, a blue metallic '59 Ford Galaxy convertible. They "hopped-up" their cars, and as teenagers were known to drag race up and down Route 21, an activity that awarded them a few points on their drivers' licenses.

Before leaving for Vietnam, they were granted home leave. All three had romantic involvements. Bill Coyne became engaged to Vickie Eisenbri, his high school sweetheart, and Tim Berry and Richie Fuchs had plans to marry upon their return. Richie purchased an engagement ring.

As the men boarded the helicopter, they did not know it but their time on earth would end in less than 1,000 heartbeats. As the craft gained altitude, it circled over the South China Sea before heading south to Quang Nagi Province. Within minutes a catastrophic engine failure caused a complete loss of power sending them plunging into the surf. Ten men perished in the crash, a crew of four and six passengers. Had the engine failed on the way in, my name would now be on the Vietnam Veterans Memorial Wall in Washington, D.C., carved on Panel 14E instead of theirs.

The Massillon Boys were all born on a Tuesday in the fall of 1946, and their lives would end that Wednesday, January 11, 1967, a few months short of their twenty-first birthdays. Also born on a Tuesday in 1946, my life and theirs converged when I arrived in Chu Lai and joined them in the 1st Shore Party Battalion.

Those of us born this year represented the leading edge of the baby boom generation that fed the massive troop build-up of 1965. Some boomers were lucky and drew better hands than the rest of us. George Bush and Bill Clinton, both born a couple of months ahead of the Massillon boys, were midway through their sophomore year at Yale and Georgetown Universities when my comrades climbed on that chopper. Donald Trump, born in June of '46, was at the University of Pennsylvania's Wharton School of Business preparing to become a multibillionaire.

But on that fateful day in 1967, the Massillon Boys drew aces and eights, their human potential and future lives gone forever. There would be no GI bill or college education to pursue. The day would never come when they could vote or legally order an alcoholic beverage. None had the chance to have children or enjoy family life. And, regrettably, Bill Coyne and Vickie Eisenbrei never walked down the aisle as husband and wife. Richie, Bill, and Tim never saw a PC, never used the Internet or cell phone, and did not see Neal Armstrong walk on the moon.

After half a century, I still remember these men and our time together in Vietnam. I wondered if any knowledge or memory of them still exists in Massillon or its institutions. I contacted the town historian who said a viaduct connecting two areas of the city carried plaques with their names as well as the other Massillon men who died in Vietnam. Dedicated in 2009, it is now the Vietnam Veterans Memorial Viaduct.

At the dedication ceremony, Richie Fuch's 1965 Dodge Coronet (remarkably it still exists) was the first car driven over, as a gesture of remembrance and respect. David Harrison, a former comrade of the 1st Shore Party Battalion, was the driver and Bill's fiancée, Tim's girlfriend, and Joe Rivera, a friend and fellow Marine, were passengers. It was a bitterly cold December day, but this did not deter those many Massillonians who came to pay tribute and respect.

I traveled to Massillon and met former members of the 1st Shore Party Battalion who served with Richie, Tim, and Bill. They were also my former comrades, but as age has transformed us, none could recognize the other. These former Marines took me to the Memorial Viaduct and to City Hall where an impressive display of statues and plaques honor the Massillonians who died defending our country.

I contacted Bill Coyne's fiancée, Tim Berry's girlfriend, and Richie's brother to inquire about their lives growing up in Massillon. They confirmed for me what I already knew from my association with them; these men had character traits we all admire: a work ethic, intelligence, moral and ethical principles, and a sense of patriotism.

David Harrison, also a NE Ohioan and friend of the Massillon Boys, was one of the Marines I reconnected with while visiting. On the day of the crash, he asked the Command Gunnery Sergeant for permission to join the mission and was turned down. Had the request been approved, his name would now be engraved on the Wall along with the others.

Days after the crash, Richie Fuch's body washed up on the beach without clothes or dog tags, and Dave was summoned to identify him. Memories flooded into his mind reminding him of happier days when the four of them hung out at the Massillon party spots, along with their girlfriends, bragging about whose car was the fastest. Now he realized he was (is) the last man standing.

Dave and I were lucky that day, drawing hands that left us with future lives denied to Bill, Richie, and Tim. Our kismets played out through fortunate circumstance as opposed to good fortune by birth.

The ones responsible for the Vietnam War: Lyndon Johnson, Robert McNamara, Ho Chi Minh, believed in Pyrrhic victories to service their manhood. The trouble with victories at all costs is that they rarely affect battalion headquarters or decision makers in capitol cities; instead they impact the individual warrior carrying the sword, arbalest, musket, or in our case M-14s. From time immemorial, societies have sent the members of their group with the least privilege and power to fight for those that have it—and so it was with Vietnam.

Two years after the crash, the rock group *Creedence Clearwater Revival* produced a hit single titled "Fortunate Son" about the disparity of war sacrifice between those with privilege and those without. Whenever I hear it, it seems so utterly relevant and stirs emotion and reflection in me about these men and their loss in that war so long ago.

Dave Harrison (left) and Richie Fuchs (right). Image courtesy of Dave Harrison.

In 1967, Ken McBride served as a United States Marine in Vietnam. He was a comrade and friend of the men from Massillon. Two weeks after their deaths, McBride was himself wounded and spent several weeks convalescing in military hospitals before being sent home. He has written for the *St. Louis Post-Dispatch*, *Massillon Independent*, *Reader's Digest*, and other publications.

Leonard Adreon

The Forgotten War: A Personal Reflection on the Korean War

Of course, it is forgotten. It ended 63 years ago. Not many of us around anymore. I came home in 1952. Even then, there was little interest in the war. In those war years there was no 24/7 channel TV news. Most people received their news on the radio or by reading the newspaper. Some people experienced glimpses of the war on fuzzy pictures on their little round television screens. I do not believe that anyone can understand war by seeing brief film or video clips.

During the three years and one month of the killing, 54,246 Americans died in Korea, including 36,574 servicemen and women killed in action. Parents, spouses, children, and friends of the 54,246 did not forget the war. Compare that to the 8,000 killed in 11 years in Afghanistan and Iraq. I only offer this for perspective. The war in Korea was intense. Every war death is terrible.

In 1952, hospitals were filled with the 103,264 wounded in Korea. In addition, 8,177 servicemen were missing in action. Today the 8,177 are still unaccounted for. Their families will never know what happened to them.

People said we lost the war. After all, when the war started on June 25, 1950, there were two Koreas divided at the 38th parallel. When the killing stopped on July 27, 1953, there were two Koreas divided at the 38th parallel. South Korea's President Syngman Rhee's goal of one democratic Korea was never realized.

What would it be like today if we hadn't fought that war? There would undoubtedly be one Korea under the leadership of Kim Jong-un. The 50 million people of South Korea would be living in misery like the sad people of North Korea.

South Korea today is a successful, thriving, and free nation. The South Koreans are a kind, compassionate people who have survived a brutal Japanese occupation and the devastation of the invasion by North Korea and the intervention of the Chinese. South Korea is a progressive, productive nation. Check your Samsung device as you drive around town in your Hyundai. Those who say we lost the war disrespect the thousands of Americans who lost an arm, a leg, an eye, or their life in the Korean War. The full story of what happened there will never be fully told. I can describe what I experienced in the early winter of 1951.

It was cold, a colorless sky, and wet. It wasn't rain. It wasn't snow. Icy pellets fell from the heavy gray. I stood at the bottom of the mountain and looked up 5,000 or 6,000 feet to the top. The pellets stung as they pummeled my face. I lowered my helmet. I couldn't see the top through the mist and fog. I knew the Chinese were there. Our orders were to take the hill.

This was the highest hill in the area. We owned it before they had driven us off the hill. From their position they could pin us down and even attack our convoys on the Main Service Road. Our command had decided that this was the perfect day to take it back. Visibility was so poor, they couldn't see us assemble for the assault. The disadvantage to the condition that day was that our Corsairs couldn't fly, so we would have no air support.

The Marines of D Company were waiting in the dark, preparing to move up. We had added extra men because we knew it would be tough. We needed more bazookas, ammo, and grenades than usual. We had to find a way to take out their machine gun nests that guarded the summit.

I was one of ten corpsmen. My carbine was loaded and ready. All of us carried an extra med pack so we would have plenty of morphine, bandages, iodine tubes, and other items needed to handle the wounded. As soon as the first light trickled through the clouds, the order was given. We started up the hill.

At first it was very quiet. The climb wasn't too bad. It was not steep but it was rocky. We had to dodge loose rocks as they cascaded down. About a third of the way up, all hell broke loose as the Chinese reacted to the assault and started firing from their dug-in positions. Visibility worsened from exploding shells. We went from silence to the constant rumble of gunfire. We would run, crawl, hit the ground, and fire at the flashes of light as our fire teams leapfrogged up the slope.

I heard the yell, "Corpsman" to my right about 30 yards above. I put my head down and followed the sound of the yell. A Marine was down, his face in the muck, not moving. A corporal and I turned him over, but the fixed stare immediately told us it was too late. He was our lead lieutenant. The corporal removed his belt and handed it to me, together with his holster and 45 caliber pistol. He said, "Doc, take this, you might need it." I was surprised, started to suggest that he take it, but before I could say anything, he had moved on. I strapped the belt around my waist.

Hour after hour, the men of my company slowly and tediously ran, crawled, and slithered through the mud inching up the saturated slope of that terrible hill. Our advance forces finally got far enough to attack their machine gun emplacements. We used bazookas, BARs, flamethrowers and grenades to try to stop the rapid firing that was taking a terrible toll on our men. Although it wasn't my job, I had a good arm from my baseball days and could throw a grenade farther than some of my Marine buddies. They were glad to have my help throwing grenades at the machine gun barricades. I felt compelled to do more than just treat the wounded. I repeatedly fired my carbine and used up most of my 30 round clips. I don't know if that helped the assault. The carbine wasn't as powerful or as accurate as the marine's M-1's. The flamethrowers finished off the job. The sight of the Chinese machine gunner running out of the barricade on fire, his face blackened by the flames, was jolting to me each time it happened. Watching him fall, his body shaking, was a brutal picture of this war. I felt better when the shaking stopped. I knew that for him the war was over.

About 8 hours after we started up the hill, we made it to the top. The Chinese had left their positions and were scurrying down the north side of the mountain. We did not follow them. Our assignment was to take and secure the hill. My fellow corpsmen and I were barely able to keep up with the needs of the wounded. We worked to the point of exhaustion. Our tasks were not finished as night descended upon the hill.

There was scant light when I treated a lone Chinese lying in a rut, his white quilted jacket splotched by blackened blood mixed with mud. He was alert. He didn't move. He looked up at me. He barely whispered, "Help me." I was surprised he spoke English. I took his helmet off. I was looking into the distressed eyes of a kid, looked like high school age to me. I opened his jacket to see the wounds. He grimaced. I placed some bandages on the area where blood was oozing from his wound. I told him to push on the bandages as hard as he could. He understood. I asked, "You speak English?"

He nodded, "A little."

I spoke slowly, "We're going to put you on a stretcher and take you off the hill."

He looked up at me with pleading eyes and asked, "Will you tell my parents I am ok?"

I said, "You can write from the POW camp after your wounds heal." I wasn't sure that was true but I said it anyway.

He smiled a tight smile and said, "Thank you."

The stretcher came. He was carried away. I can't forget his painful wave to me. I don't know if he made it. I hope he did.

That was the worse single assault for our company during my time with them. Two hundred and forty of us started up the hill. Eighty-seven made it to the top. We owned the hill. We paid too much.

The war in Korea never ended. Only a cease-fire, called an armistice, was agreed to in July of 1953. In 2009, the North Koreans unilaterally rejected that agreement. In March 2013, North Korea announced that it was scrapping all non-aggression pacts with South Korea. Today, the Demilitarized Zone (DMZ) near the 38th parallel is the most heavily defended national border in the world. The United States has more than 30,000 troops stationed in Korea.

I find it disturbing that, after 63 years, the Korean peninsula is poised for a continuation of the war that never ended.

Leonard J. Adreon is from St. Louis, Missouri. He was in the U.S. Navy from 1944 to 1946 and a corpsman with the First Marine Division in combat in Korea in 1951–1952. He is a graduate of Washington University in St. Louis, married, has three daughters, and six grandchildren. He recently completed a new book, *Hilltop Doc, A Marine Corpsman Fighting Through the Mud and Blood of the Korean War.*

A. Sean Taylor

Always Time For Chai

Captain A. Sean Taylor, PAO, 649th RSG, United States Army Reserve, Cedar Rapids, IA, enlisted with the Iowa Army National Guard on October 24, 2002, at the age of 35. He deployed to Bagram, Afghanistan, with the Iowa Guard from 2010–2011 and just recently returned in 2015 from a deployment to Taji, Iraq, with the 310th ESC Advise and Assist Team, supporting the Iraqi Security Forces with their fight against ISIS/ISIL.

Jarrod L. Taylor

Innocence Reflected

Jarrod L. Taylor served as an infantryman in the U.S. Army from 2000–2009. During that time, he deployed to Uzbekistan and Afghanistan in 2001–2002, Horn of Africa in 2003, Afghanistan in 2004–2005, and Iraq from 2007–2009. He received a BA in History from Eastern Illinois University in 2013, and he currently resides in Shelbyville, Kentucky, with his wife and two children.

Journey Carolyn Collins

Forgiven Too

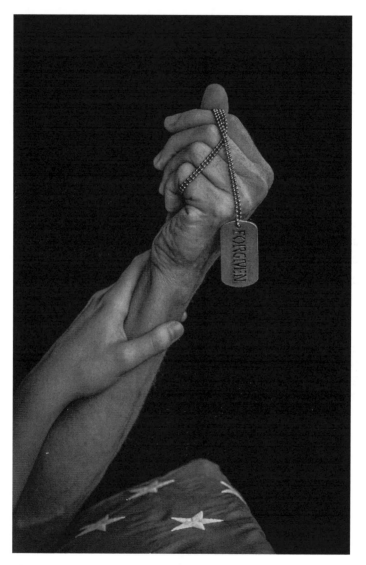

Journey Carolyn Collins is 13 years old and took this picture of her grandpa, a Vietnam war veteran. In school, she learned about Vietnam, and her teacher told her the brutal truth about what had happened. Before Vietnam, her grandpa said if he came back alive he would buy a new Wilson T2000 tennis racket. Recently he gave this tennis racket to her. Even if he doesn't think so, she knows that her grandpa is a true hero.

Bill Glose

Questions Raised by Black Scorpions

Where they came from, no one knew, these segmented,
scabrous creatures we had to shake from our boots.
So foreign-seeming to us foreigners, who thought
we were anything but.

Who was first to snap them up in Tupperware? I can't recall.
Only the way each backed away with pincers raised,
tail curled into a venom-spiked question mark.

What we did was place two of them in circles
inscribed by ammo crates and watched them fight.

Which would live and which would die? We bet on them
instead of looking at ourselves, letters we'd written
"just in case" burning like coals in our pockets.

When orders sent us scuttling into Iraq, we set them free
and oiled our weapons' moving parts. Each man
swimming in an ocean of questions he wanted to ask.
Leaders pointed out destinations on maps inscribed with
grease-marker circles. Only answer we would ever get.

Bill Glose is a former paratrooper and author of three poetry collections, including *Half a Man*, whose poems arise from his experiences as a combat platoon leader in the Gulf War.

Bryan D. Nickerson

Runaway Slave

Twenty clicks as the crow flies
in the impenetrable terrain of central Afghanistan.
You fled your home one September evening

in the clothes of a Taliban Commander, your husband.
The cover of darkness protecting you.

Your sky-blue burka, hidden in the brush
outside your village once you slipped away,
the blue bars through which you saw the world.

Forced to walk behind a man and
turn away and kneel should another approach.

Should night fail you, you would have
been returned to your Commander and killed,
but only after he beat you,

raped you until you wished for death.
The end would be in sight though,

as opposed to the unknown number of years
since you became his young property.
A lifetime of being passed around,

a fucktoy to your Master's comrades.
Repeatedly sodomized and beaten

for any reason they deemed appropriate.
You reach our gate at 0300
in desperate need of medical attention.

Parched lips, sunken facial features,
swollen abdomen that could only be a child.

Looking for a way out.

We couldn't turn you away, we took you in,
a grievous offense in your culture.

You relayed the story of your pre-arranged prison.
We contacted Headquarters and asked to evacuate you

in the hopes you could start anew,
someplace far away from your slave master.
In the heat of early dawn

we hid you underneath a blanket
and carried you on a stretcher

to the landing zone. A Blackhawk
touched down in a whirlwind
of dirt and stones.

Then through the tornado of
stinging dirt and debris you

were raised up and carried off
to a place we would never know
to what I hope would be a better life.

Bryan D. Nickerson was born in Buffalo, New York. He dropped out of college in 2007 to enlist in the Army and served from July 2007 until January 2015. He served as an Airborne Infantryman for one tour in Iraq and three in Afghanistan. Nickerson held most positions from squad leader and below. He has reentered college. He writes out of North Carolina with the love and support of his wife, Laura.

Milton J. Bates

First Blood

Bien Hoa Air Base, 1970

From where they stood it had a jaunty look,
rocking from side to side like a bus full
of restless children. They'd ridden others
like it to school and summer camp, but this
was olive drab, not orange-yellow, and rigged
with window grates to fend off hand grenades.

The airport shuttle carried troops both ways,
some to war, others to a Freedom Bird
back home. The new arrivals wondered why
the home-bound bus would creep so slowly
toward their stop. And why was the driver
hunkered low behind the wheel, his face
a mask of terror? Before the folding door
could spill its secret, they heard pounding feet
and someone shouting, *Make a hole! Stand back!*

The MPs went to work with their batons,
then dragged the brawlers from the bus, handcuffed
and sullen. Blood clotted in their hair and stained
their fatigues. These children hadn't learned
how to play or kill together, black and white.

The newbies climbed aboard and took their seats
in silence. War comes in many colors,
they were thinking, not just the green on green
whose uniform they wore, whose *how* they
understood, if not its *why*. Now they knew
they hadn't left that other war behind,
the one in which their skin enlisted them.

Milton J. Bates served as an army sergeant in Vietnam in 1970–1971. He is the author of several nonfiction books, including *The Wars We Took to Vietnam: Cultural Conflict and Storytelling* (University of California Press, 1996). His poems have appeared in various anthologies and magazines. Five Oaks Press will publish his poetry chapbook, *Always on Fire,* in 2016.

Tessa Poppe

A Bird

So it always is: when you escape to a desert the silence shouts in your ear.
—Graham Greene, *The Quiet American*

What sticks to memory, often, are those odd little fragments that have no beginning and no end. . .
—Tim O'Brien, *The Things They Carried*

It was an abnormally humid day for late October when I found a bird outside my window. It was lying there amongst the potted plants gone cold from an earlier, forgotten frost. It was wide-eyed and still, its only movement, a feathery grey chest rising and falling. I found it when I went to open the window, thinking how obscenely warm it was inside the house. It was an unsettling heat, with the leaves all orange and red, the sun so bright, like we were all about to become the victims of a fast approaching flame. But I stopped thinking about that when I saw the bird. It was bigger than a sparrow and smaller than a dove. I've never been much of a bird-watcher so I couldn't call it by name, but I became mystified by the flying creature, now airless and trapped by earth.

I had a lot of plans for that day, a to-do list: groceries and emails and bills stacking up on the end table, but now I couldn't stop staring and wondering and dreaming about this bird. Its state of paralysis disturbed me. But I decided to move on with my day, leaving it there in the dirt, secretly hoping it would get up and fly away or go peacefully into death's sleep.

I started cleaning. I started picking up, even though that was not in my plans. After a while, I stopped dusting and went to look at the bird. It was still there. Chest rising and falling, rising and falling. I went back to work. I folded clothes. I vacuumed. I scrubbed the sink in the bathroom, breaking a sweat. Bleached the toilet. Mopped the kitchen floor. Swept the porch. And as I went along doing mindless things I wondered if God knew that one of His creatures had fallen. Was He up there coaxing it home? Was He watching it suffer? I felt sick. I went to the bleached toilet and threw up. I stopped cleaning. I got a towel to wrap the bird in. I went outside and looked into its eyes. I wondered why it chose my dead flowers to die in. Did he know I would find him?

We were walking home from dinner in December, what year it was I can't recall, sometime after we both left the Army. But I remember the minutes that ticked by, the conversation, the way our breath lingered in the cold air for a minute, the way you kept walking all funny, stumbling into the snow. I remember feeling my hands beginning to numb, I'd forgotten my gloves and it was six blocks back to my apartment. It seemed like every house along that college-town street had blinking red lights and a Santa out front.

I cried all afternoon and didn't know why. I wanted to tell you, I figured you'd think I was mad even though I knew you cried too sometimes, but for different reasons.

You turned around and stared at me for a moment before lighting a cigarette. I know you saw it on me, that afternoon's tear-stains on my cheeks, even though they weren't there anymore. The memory sticks to my brain like the strand of hair you couldn't get out of your mouth at dinner.

There was only blinking red on white snow and us standing there, looking at each other. You took your time, probably deciding whether or not you should say something. The cigarette wouldn't light, so you pulled your hood up and cussed. I came closer to you, to help shield the cigarette with my cold hands and had the impulse to say something, anything that would change the subject from where it was going to go. I hated your seeing me weak. I noticed the mascara running down your cheeks, your eyes watering due to the freezing temperature, so I tried erasing it with my thumb, but only managed to smudge it further.

You finally got it lit and I watched a plow truck go by, pushing snow onto all the parked cars. I wondered how you'd bring it up.

"You think too hard."

"You don't think hard enough," I said, and you laughed.

"Yeah, maybe. You're sensitive though," and you looked down like you didn't want to say that, but as if it explained everything at the same time. An explanation: a cure.

Oh thank God, that's what I've been looking for, I thought to myself sarcastically, but didn't say it out loud. Instead I said, "And you feel nothing." There was a bottle of wine between us, this made saying it easier. But my words were sharp and I think they cut you.

"Al-ice," you said my name slowly as if you were trying to wake me up without scaring me. "There's nothing you could do."

But I had already accepted that there really was something I could have done for that boy, that day in the mountains. I should not be free, walking around at night and going to dinners.

Anger rested on my face. My face felt hot in the bitter cold. I think I might have been angry at you, for making me feel crazy, like I had made something up to be sad about.

"It's that place, that's how it is. They're animals."

I looked down at my fleece boots. Let it go. I wanted to drown.

"We were there to help people," I said.

"It's all bullshit. It's all lies that got us there."

It is now a memory.

* * *

I left the bird to die and went back inside to sit at my desk and pay bills. I studied my reflection in the screen. I sat there staring long enough that the monitor went black. I thought I looked older than I should, my collar bone protruded more, when was the last time I ate? I took off my glasses and leaned into the screen, the blackness made it easier to see myself. My brown hair looked greasy and my face seemed tired. Not enough sleep.

Suddenly I felt my heart pounding in my chest, there was a heat rising with its pounding—up from my stomach and into my throat. There must be a rock in there, a rock that was suddenly catching on fire. Rocks don't catch on fire. I went into the bathroom. My throat was hoarse from all the throwing up. That must be it. I opened my mouth in the mirror and looked and saw nothing. I wanted to reach my hand in and pull it out. What was it, what was that? I thought I recognized it, that thing. It was guilt; no, sorrow. An aching, but it felt like a heavy weight and steel and fire. I wanted to see it sitting in the back of my throat where my tonsils were. Something left behind to fester.

* * *

"I want to forget," I told you.

"You will. Eventually." There was sincerity in your voice although your words fell flat.

Why do I rely on words? Have they lost their meaning too? Honor. Duty. Sacrifice. Yellow. Blue. Airplane. Table. Letter. Tea. Light. Vase. Granite. Love. Cockroach. Rape. Dirt.

"I feel as though I'm a different person now, don't you get that?" I can't remember if I actually said this or not.

I wished that night to be the last we spoke of it because we didn't speak of it anyway. The memory of us is a picture in my head that I pull up from time to time, of you walking away, into the darkness, your dark green coat pulled up close to your neck. You held it shut and didn't use the zipper. Your long, blond hair came out around your neck.

I expected you to turn around and say something. But you were never really good at making an effort. Sometimes I thought it was because you didn't care; now I know it's because you didn't know how.

"Lucy."

You threw your hand up in response, the one holding a cigarette, as if waving me off to some unknown end.

"When will we be out of the woods?" I asked.

"When that flag drapes over our casket, baby."

At this I smiled because I could hear the brevity in your voice, that short, abrupt, and comical end to what was only dreary and sad, a storm cloud lingering over a mountain valley. A valley a part of me still existed in, the one with the constant hum of helicopters, generators, brief mortar attacks, but most nights a quiet so loud—it made me numb.

In that moment I forgave you for not giving a damn, because I knew if we both felt it, the thing, we'd fall into that valley and never come out.

* * *

I went back to the bird for the second time and felt its feathers on my skin. My fingertips tingled. I noticed his eyes now. They were darting to and fro, two little black diamonds. I saw nothing and everything in them. That's not possible. I wept. I felt its dying on me and soon it was coming out in my breath. I was inhabited by a cry. What is wrong with you? Stop crying.

I picked him up and felt his cold, stiff body in my bare, clammy hands, as if he were already dead. The fragility of his caged chest in my palm made me uneasy. I expected him to be warm, like the ground I stood on, like the air around me, but his coldness startled me, and I dropped him on the ground covered in fire or leaves. I looked down and for a second I couldn't see the grey body amongst all the orange. I was scared to move, afraid I would step on him. I thought of that small chest snapping, the sound of twigs breaking echoed in my ears. I thought of Lucy, she'd be laughing at me. You care too much. She always knew something I didn't, the insignificance of things.

* * *

Everything was dead, but those black diamonds. I can see you want to live. I meant to say that to the bird, but I said it to myself.

"Why are you here?" I asked him out loud. "You must have come from somewhere." Fallen out of the sky, a warning. I noticed how sweaty I was. I took off my sweatshirt. I took off my socks and stood in all the orange and red leaves, against the white painted house in my bare feet. The heat was still on me, in me, and in my throat, not rope but barbed wire. This was the thing. The thing was memory so acute that it had physical characteristics. It crawled. It burned. It was a shape. The thing defined me now and propelled me toward what end, I didn't know.

I set the bird on the kitchen table, wrapped in a white towel, his chest still rising and falling. His eyes were now wild and scared. They had always been wild, I thought, but now they were scared. I imagined he was trying to move but was paralyzed. I imagined his whole life and what it had been, all the things he must have seen from above the tree-tops. How had such a bird fallen? And why did it matter? It didn't matter. I was just born with a bruise, so things hurt.

* * *

This is what it is to watch something suffer. I had done it once before. It was also a grotesquely hot day, sweat pooling at the base of my spine, at the crooks of my elbows and backs of my knees. Everything was so heavy on my back, on my hips, on my feet. My feet burned. It's just a bird, it's just a bird, it's just a bird. There's no morality in this.

* * *

"Alice. How is the thing?" you asked, never saying it but standing on its edge, on my edge, as if I were an abyss you might fall into. Don't stand too close.

How long has it been, since we spoke? There were months between us. And many, many miles. We were on your porch, back home in the country. You weren't wearing any makeup and I held a coffee mug with iced tea in it. I grew silent and wanted to hide the thing and myself from you, but you were always good at finding me.

I was on one of those brief trips home where we went out of our way to spend time together, knowing all the while the things we would not talk about, but wanted to. Our lives were a play we acted in, the curtains never closing. The deployments were in the background, as if we were on a stage and they were set pieces behind us, coloring a land-scape we pretended not to notice. Inherent structures to our lives.

"What is the thing?" I pretended it disappeared somewhere between time and space, an afterthought I'd left on the side of the road.

You avoided naming it. "How are you doing?"

"Doesn't really matter."

"It matters every bit," and you squeezed my hand. But it didn't matter. You didn't really want me to talk about it. The thing was heat, the thing was a mass and at the same time it was a crevice, a space.

"Are you happy here?" I asked to avoid all conversation on the matter, but curious. You didn't flinch. You had become complacent on that porch, in that house, yet we still looked at one another like two people who saw the cracks in each other that no one else did.

"You can't hold onto it though, you'll disappear. Time will pass and you'll be better, we all will," you said.

I didn't believe you.

I wondered if you thought you were doing better than before. I wanted to tell you about it but at the same time your presence made the thing smaller. I felt like it would separate us even more, for you to know all of it, the everything. This was the last time I uttered a word about that day in Afghanistan. The day I saw a boy get raped and looked away.

I had stood watch throughout the night. The sun was just rising over the Pakistani mountains, and with it, the morning's humidity came to rest on my skin. The valley in front of me looked purple. And I rubbed my eyes to keep awake. It was then that I noticed a young man and the little boy next to a house, nothing more than a brick and mortar construction that probably consisted of one room. It was not too far from my guard position. They didn't know I could see them. He had taken the boy out behind the house, and at first I couldn't understand what they were doing. It was light outside, but barely, and it seemed out of place that they were there, hiding like that, so I looked through my scope and studied them. I soon dropped my weapon to my side and just stood there. I envisioned raising it again and shooting the man in the head. My fingers twitched as if my body wanted to do it but my head said not to. I wondered if I'd get court-martialled, I wondered if I'd accidentally shoot the boy, I wondered if it was his brother or his father. I got sick and threw up at my feet. I looked up and they were still there at the side of the house. That's when the man noticed me and stopped. I wondered if he'd heard me vomit. He left the boy to stand there by himself outside. The boy looked down at the ground for some time. I noticed his bare feet. He couldn't have been more than seven or eight. I wondered how often he was taken out behind the house like that. I half expected him to look over at me but he didn't. He walked off, down through a grove of trees and out onto the only paved road in the province that went in front of our camp. He just kept walking up that road towards the village market,and I watched him until he disappeared.

I didn't tell anyone for a while. I hadn't done the right thing . . . anything. I watched a child get raped, but those exact words never passed

48

my lips. Maybe I didn't do anything because I didn't give a shit at the end of the day. When I told Lucy, she said I couldn't have shot that man. She stood to remind me of those rules of engagement that dictated everything we could and couldn't do. There was a large part of me that wished I'd shot him anyway or screamed or threw something, anything but stand there in silence.

"And what would it matter in the end, Alice? That's the way things are here," she said. And she wasn't wrong. Wasn't this just the banality of it all? This war, this place, and our place in it? I went about my days telling myself I didn't care and it didn't matter to the point I forgot about it. But it didn't go far. After I came home, it crept up and felt like a well of space in me, a blackness that spread towards, me and I couldn't tell if it was water coming to drown me or nothing at all. It was never the mortars or IEDs that kept me up at night. I prepared myself for those things. I did not prepared myself for this.

* * *

The bird's wings moved. Was he trying to get away? Was he trying to live? No, it was something awful, something else. I just stood over him and stared down. I wasn't quite sure if I was in my kitchen anymore. "It will be okay," I said, but it was useless. I felt ridiculous saying it, but all the while feeling grief. I mourned something, was it me? Was I already so far out to sea that I couldn't come back? I imagined Lucy standing on a beach, calling me back, but I had no desire to swim to her.

* * *

"I'm sorry," I said to the bird. He looked right at me. I stroked him lightly with my index finger. He must have been lying there all night, suffocating in those dead flowers by my window, hoping I'd see. I didn't see. I looked at other things, but not the bird. I ignored it even. My tears fell on his smooth feathers, beading up and rolling off. His chest did not rise and fall as quickly. His eyes were less wild.

Tessa Poppe grew up in the Midwest where she served in the Iowa Army National Guard, deploying to Iraq in 2007 and Afghanistan in 2010. She currently works at the U.S. Institute of Peace in Washington, D.C., and holds a Master's Degree in Security Studies from Georgetown University. Tessa writes non-fiction, short stories, and poetry. Her work has appeared in *34th Parallel Magazine*, *0-Dark Thirty*, *Task and Purpose*, and *Foreign Policy's Best Defense* column.

Kyle Larkin

Into Dust

A sandstorm is coming. I can't see the clouds yet, but a faint, gritty mist is beginning to permeate the city. It's almost imperceptible, except for the tiny grains of sand accumulating in the corners of my mouth and eyes, crunching between my teeth, and leaving a thin layer of dust over everything. We received word from one of the bases that it's moving toward us—a real monster of a storm, they said. Could last for days.

I trace a few shapes in the dust with my finger, waiting for the massive wall of sand to roll in like a tidal wave and block out all of the light. Sometimes the storms let up just enough for everything to be covered in an eerie, hazy orange glow, making it somehow both light and dark at once, like being too close to a forest fire. But when they're really bad, you can't see anything at all. You can't hear anything at all.

"The sand will never come out," Sage once said as we sat shoulder-to-shoulder in the back of a dusty truck, rolling down an endless desert highway with nothing but sand as far as we could see in every direction. He turned toward me and shouted it again over the noise of the engine, making sure I heard him. "The sand will never come out!" I nodded and pretended to adjust my rifle sling. "Never," he continued. "It's part of us now, always will be, and we are part of *it* now," he said, eyes wide behind his goggles. "We just have to accept that." We rode along, watching out the back of the truck as trails of dust stretched out far behind the tires and into the distance, lingering in the air for a long time. He pulled his scarf down to speak clearer. "It's in our hair, it's under our nails, it's behind our ears, it's *inside* our damn ears. It cakes up our eyes; we're constantly wiping and picking at crusted sand. We blow our noses and brown, snotty mud comes out. It's in our food. Our mouths always feel gritty. We breathe in thick clouds of dust, and it fills our nostrils and mouths," he said, pausing to gesture toward the sand hanging in the air of the covered truck bed where we sat. "It goes down our throats and into our lungs. It travels through our bronchioles, through our alveoli and into our bloodstreams, into our organs. We eat it, we breathe it, we digest it, we piss and shit sand. It's part of us now, and it'll never come out, I'm telling you," he said, grinning. "It's even in our bones!" Then he pulled his scarf back over his face and we continued staring out the back of the truck, watching the desert sands stretch on forever.

Sometimes it's coarse and rough and abrasive, other times it's fine and smooth, and yet it can also be a filmy dust that seems more like smoke, but what exactly is in this sand that is becoming part of us? The locals say that the desert is nature's crematory, and, if that's true, then this sand is the ashes of worlds long gone, the crumbs left over from monuments and castles, the remains of once-great cities, the remains of mediocre and failed cities. It's the weathered bone dust of people and animals and plants and bugs and stone and metal and trash and chemicals and blood and waste and filth. It's the residue of all that has come and gone and returned to ashes and dust. Everything is in this sand.

I trace a few more shapes in the dust as the wind picks up. It won't be long now. The mist is becoming more noticeable; I can feel the grains hit against my cheek, and it's starting to appear dark far off in the distance. I sit and wait.

The wall of sand itself is enormous. When it first comes into sight, its sheer size gives the impression that it's not even moving, and the only way to tell that the storm is heading toward me is that I notice less of the city than I could see before. Buildings begin to disappear— palm trees, entire blocks vanish, mosques and minarets are swallowed up, creating an optical illusion where it seems like the city is moving toward the cloud, rather than the other way around, as if the storm is a sort of vortex, a swirling quicksand black hole that is sucking everything into it.

I put on my goggles, pull my scarf over my face, and wait. The hazy orange glow comes on quickly. I can barely make out the edge of the roof, or the boards and sandbags around me. Standing up and moving around is like groping through a dimly lit attic or stepping outside into the darkness of night before your eyes have adjusted. I grab my rifle and sit back down, laying it across my lap.

The roaring rush of sand grows louder. I raise my hand directly in front of my face, knowing that I won't be able to see it, but I do it anyway and am amazed just the same. How can there be this much sand in the air? It doesn't seem real. I clap my hands hard and feel them connect, but I don't hear their sound. For a long time, I sit still with my face covered, trying to comprehend the phenomenon that is this storm. It can't stay this heavy the whole time, there's no way; it's probably only this bad in the beginning. I think about shooting a round into the air, just to see what happens. Nobody would hear it anyway, which again makes me consider how useless it is for me to be sitting up here. If something were to happen, if I started shooting off entire cans of ammo—assuming the guns would even fire—nobody would know.

I turn, using my back to block the sand as I hunch over the radio, and try to call up for a check. I put the receiver directly against my ear but hear nothing. I pull my shirt up over my head and bring the radio underneath to try calling again. There is the faint but recognizable squealing beep, but it sounds far away, and then I don't hear anything else.

I try sitting in different positions so that I breathe in less of the dust. I put my head down, face my chair in opposite directions, try to block the sand by covering the doorway with my poncho, but none of this helps. The poncho seems to work for a moment, but sand creeps in from every possible crevice and opening. Besides that, it traps the sand inside the walls rather than letting it blow through, so I take it back down. I keep wiping the front of my goggles out of habit, even though it makes no difference and I can't see anything. Sand is up my sleeves, on my neck, down my shirt, sticking to my sweaty skin.

The storm sounds like a giant waterfall, but its tiny grains also blot out all of the other sound waves travelling through the air, creating a bizarre sort of white noise that is both deafening and muting. I wonder what the guys at the other positions are thinking about or if any of them have decided to test their rifles against the noise of the sand. I wouldn't know if they were in trouble, either. We're all just sitting and waiting. I think about the guys who aren't out on positions right now, lying in their bunks, trying to keep the sand out of our little room. I think about how our door doesn't shut all the way, so during sandstorms we tape garbage bags around the cracks and stuff blankets against the bottom. I think about how this never works because the sand always gets in anyway, and as soon as it seems like whatever amount of sand that has blown into the room is beginning to settle, the door flies open and someone walks in yelling the way a person with loud music in their headphones yells when they talk, because they're coming in from the deafening, muting sand; and I think about how, for a split second when the door is open, the light catches all of the sand pouring in, and you can see the air thick with it, can see it move as you breathe it in and out, can see the millions of tiny grains just hanging in the air, as if they're permanent; and I think about how everyone yells and swears and throws things at whoever let in all of the sand and messed up the intricate layout of protective garbage bags and blankets, which they now have to replace in their exact positions; and I think about how nobody sincerely gets angry because everyone knows it's better to be sitting in a sandy room than to be out on missions getting blown to pieces. I think about how everyone then goes right back to lying in their bunks and waiting for the sand to settle enough to start talking again, at least until the next person bursts in, and how once the sand gets bad enough in there, and enough time has gone by for them to stop caring about most things, they will start smoking cigarettes in that little room, since it's already filled with sand anyway and they sure as hell aren't going outside, so what difference does it make?

When my replacement comes tomorrow morning, I will climb down the ladder, feeling my way like a blind person, walk over to our shack, open the door and get yelled at, replace the blankets that I pushed out of place when I opened the door, make my way to my bunk, lie under my sheets, and try to breathe normally until the storm has ended and we have to begin cleaning. The sand and dirt and dust always accumulate like snow. We will take everything to the center of the room—all of our gear, our clothes, boots, food, books and magazines, laptops, blankets and pillows, and shake the sand out of it all as best we can, forming a giant pile. Then we will sweep it out and spend the rest of the day cleaning weapons.

I try to check the time, but there's too much sand in the air. I go underneath my shirt again and press the button on the side of my watch so it lights up. In the dull green glow I can see sand in the space between my shirt and my skin, and sand sticking to me, forming mud with the sweat. I'm hungry, but decide to wait until the storm eases up to try eating. I swing my hand back and forth along the side of my chair until I find a bottle of water. I twist open the top, trying to shield the bottle as much as possible, and pull down my scarf to take a few big gulps. Then I quickly replace the cap, spit out some of the sand that got in my mouth, and pull my scarf back up.

The only good thing about all of this sand is the cover that it provides. For once, I can finally escape the constant feeling of being watched. When we go out on a foot patrol, each of us understands that it may be his last, that we can be seen from every building, that each window is like an eye. When we go out on convoys, each of us realizes that we are being watched, that the road could erupt at any moment. On clear days, when I look out at the streets, the buildings, the alleys, and the countless windows, I know that the people in those places might also be looking at me. I feel it in my gut. So a small part of me is always flinching, maybe just internally, but flinching just the same, the way people instinctively cringe when a gun is pointed at them.

Of course, we aren't the only ones who constantly feel the angst of being watched. The people of this city understand the sensation as well. Whenever someone steps outside, they know that we watch them walk down the street, that we watch their kids play outside, that we watch their homes, that we watch them drive their cars. They know we have loaded guns pointed toward the city at all times—they only have to look up to see all of the plywood shacks on rooftops across the city, like the one I'm in right now, covered in sandbags and camouflage netting with a few black barrels pointed ominously out toward them—and I imagine that they are always flinching, too.

This creates an uncomfortable panoptical dynamic. We watch everyone, and no individual ever knows whether we are looking directly at them at any given time or not. But they also watch us, and we never know whether someone is looking directly at us at any given time or not. Both sides are simultaneously watcher and watched, causing a prolonged tension throughout the city that is as thick as the clouds of this storm. But the sand erases this dynamic—for once, nobody watches anyone. The sand makes all of us blind.

Being blind, there is no point sitting in the chair that overlooks my sector, so I move down to the floor, wedging my back into a corner, and I contemplate the staggering absurdity of my situation: I'm at an observation post, but I can't observe anything; I'm defending this position, but I'm unable to use any of the weapons to defend myself; I'm up here as a display of force and presence, but nobody can see me, nobody knows I'm present. I move around some more, trying different corners, but it's all sand.

How much sand can a person breathe and consume? There has to be a limit. I saw a movie about the first desert war, where a guy gets sick during a nightmare and leans over the sink to vomit, but sand just pours and pours out of his mouth. Will I have dreams like that? I take another few gulps of water and fumble with the cap as I try to replace it. I consider putting on my gas mask to sift some of the dust out of the air, but it's hard enough to breathe through one of those things without sand clogging up the filter. I put my head back inside my shirt and take a few deep breaths, checking my watch again. The glow seems extremely bright this time, and I realize that I haven't seen any sign of the orange haze for a few hours. I wonder whether or not the sun is still in the sky. It has probably set by now. I sit for a long time, not thinking about anything in particular, futilely trying to block the sand and to breathe as little as possible.

I try the radio again, but I can't even hear the squealing beep this time. The guys in the radio room must have given up on the checks by now—it's probably quiet in there, aside from the sounds of coffee brewing and anxious pen-clicking—and maybe they're worried, too. Why not just bring in the weapons and head back out to the positions once things clear up?

I wonder what Sage would say about the idiocy of this entire situation. Sage, whose musings about us becoming the sand and the sand becoming us became jarringly prophetic after a roadside bomb went off directly underneath his feet, and he very literally became the sand. There was a giant cloud of ash and dust, but not much else. An instantaneous cremation. Maybe he's part of the dust in this storm. Maybe I'm breathing him in right now. The explosion was so big, so unexpected; it was meant for a vehicle. We were walking along and suddenly he turned into nothing, vanished before our eyes. It didn't seem possible. Young Mueller ran around in a confused panic looking for Sage, saying that he had to be somewhere, that he must be somewhere, that he needed to find him, that Sage needed our help, that we all had to look, and why weren't we helping him look, before we finally had to grab Mueller and hold him until he collapsed in tears and loud sobs. And what do you tell a family back home after their loved one has been blown into a cloud of dust for no good reason? That his death was somehow for our country, or that it was brave and heroic, that it was for the freedom of everyone back home? I don't know what you tell them; I'm not the one who rings those doorbells or makes those phone calls.

I'm not sure what Sage would say about all of this, but he told me once that when things were bad, he would think about how the stuff we usually worry about the most doesn't really matter. "I don't mean that nihilistically," he said; "it's not *choosing* to think that things don't matter, but just sort of realizing that they don't, whether you want them to or not. It isn't a good or bad thing; it's just the way it is. Of course things matter to us, but they don't *matter*, at least not outside of us." He crouched down, pushed some sand around with his hand, and then stood up, holding out a tiny speck on his fingertip. "If our sun was the size of this grain of sand, then the next closest star would be miles away. And that's just the *closest* star. There are billions of stars in our galaxy alone, which is only one galaxy among billions of others. You might as well try to count all the grains of sand in this desert. We can't even fathom these numbers, and the idea that we, or that our planet, or that our lives are somehow the center of meaning is a cruel illusion. We can't possibly grasp or even contextualize the depth of our insignificance." I told him those were some strange things to think about when you're feeling down, but he said no, that it's comforting to know that you aren't the center of anything, and to just be a part like everything else, like this sand.

Mueller was quiet in the weeks after Sage was killed, and we worried about him, but when he finally spoke, he said he was going east as soon as our deployment was finished. "Sage told me about these monks," he said, "and they just sit up in the mountains all day long making giant patterns and designs out of tiny grains of colored sand, real intricate stuff. They spend days and weeks on them, putting each grain in just the right spot, using little tweezers and magnifying glasses and everything. And then one day they decide their project is done, and they dump the whole thing into a stream, just like that" he said, brushing off his hands, "and it's finished. That's what I'm going to do."

"More fucking sand?" someone asked him. "Haven't you played in the sand enough for one lifetime?" Mueller went quiet again, briefly, before he repeated himself, "That's what I'm going to do."

I don't know how much sand is enough for one lifetime, but when I lean back against the sandbags in this shack and feel the plastic mesh, I think of all the hours we spent filling thousands of these things and I know I'm probably close to the limit for my lifetime. In our first few months over here, we would go out on our regular missions and patrols, but then come back to fill sandbags for hours. Eventually, we built a wooden apparatus that held ten large, orange road cones upside down. One person would hold a sandbag underneath the narrow opening at the bottom of a cone, while another dug and shoveled sand into the wide opening on top, funneling it into the bag. The entire area around our filling station immediately turned into a cloud of dust once we started digging. When the bags were full, we'd tie them, load them into wheelbarrows, and stack them on the side of our building.

We breathed in the sand for hours, and the sun would get hotter as we worked. Eventually, someone would mention how nice it would be if we could just wear some goddamn shorts for once, instead of pants and boots and long sleeves and body armor and helmets, and we would all agree, but lethargically, because it's only one of those things that people say just to say it, and we all knew that we wouldn't be wearing any goddamn shorts for a long time.

The only sounds came from the metal of our e-tools scraping into the sand, sharp and violent and quick, followed by the slow whooshing and sifting of the sand being poured into the bags. Scrape, pour, scrape, pour. Sometimes Campbell would sing "Go Down Moses," or "Swing Low, Sweet Chariot," or "Down in the River to Pray," as we worked, until someone would yell for him to shut the fuck up, and we would all laugh. After a few hours, we would trudge over to the pyramid of sandbags we'd just finished filling and form a long chain that snaked up onto the roof, passing bag after bag, sweating. I would turn to my left to grab a sandbag, turn to my right to hand it off, and by the time I turned back to my left there would be another one waiting. Grab, pass, grab, pass. It was so monotonous, so hot during those weeks, and everyone was tense and angry because we were exhausted and hardly ever slept. Sometimes we would get mortared while working and have to jump down behind the piles of sandbags we'd just filled, and when it was over, we would get up and start filling them again.

One extremely hot day, we had been stacking sandbags on the roof for hours in total silence, sweating through our clothes, when Reinhardt asked, "Did you know that dry sand weighs one hundred pounds per cubic foot?" He'd barely finished this question when Thompsen threw down a sandbag and punched Reinhardt in the side of the face, knocking him over backwards. "I don't wanna hear any more about the fucking sand!" he yelled.

Then there were the hesco barriers: collapsible wire mesh boxes that are large enough to stand inside of, lined with thick cloth. We had no apparatus to help with filling these, so we just dug and poured. It was terrible work, and it took hours for two men to fill a single barrier. After weeks of struggling through sleep deprivation, we had filled a single row of them alongside our building.

Then one day some of the engineers unexpectedly showed up with front loaders and filled hundreds of the barriers within a few hours. We felt no anger, but rather shared a sort of Kantian sublime moment as we watched the tractors effortlessly filling those containers that we had sweated and struggled for so long to fill. We stood on the rooftop in awe, as if we were watching the earth itself being created. They even moved and stacked the barriers into neat walls, like they were toy blocks. We eyed every load of sand, silently trying to convert how many hundreds of shovelfuls were in each scoop, how many hours of work; and we all stared as the sand was then poured into the barriers, overflowing down the sides. We stood quietly watching this and smoking cigarettes, dumbfounded, thinking, *damn*.

At the end of those long days spent in the sand and the hot sun, digging and pouring and filling, we would trudge back to the building with our bodies covered in dust, looking like the people who walked away from Ground Zero. Once we got to our room, I would drop my armor, hang my shirt on the bunk post, peel off my boots and socks, and sleep for two or three hours before I would have to wake up, put on clean socks, cough up some sand and blow the mud out of my nose, and then decide whether my uniform could make it through the day or if I should risk soiling another one. This depended on what day it was, and how long we had to wait for the truck that took our laundry to and from the bases. Sometimes when we woke up our uniforms were still damp with sweat from the previous day, and sometimes they were dried stiff, as if starched, with giant white rings of salt deposits left behind from the evaporated sweat. If they were stiff and dry, they could be worn again, but if they were still wet, then you had to make a tough decision. And then we would start another day and do it all over again, trudging back out into the sand.

The sandbags all around our building and our rooftop positions are covered with bullet holes and rips from shrapnel, so I guess they've served their purpose, and in one place there is even a rocket propelled grenade that didn't detonate, lodged into one of the hesco barriers. I feel along the sandbags behind me, and then get up to look around, but it's still just sand everywhere. Rather than letting up, the dust seems to have grown thicker. I try the radio again, but it's all static. My mouth is full of sand and my throat is sore, so I reach for my bottle, but I mistakenly left its cap off and the contents have turned to sludge. Anxiety gradually accumulates in me along with the sand. I think that maybe I'm not getting enough air, that I'm slowly suffocating, and finally I decide to put on my gas mask.

I sit back down in the corner for a while, wondering what would happen if we were attacked right now. I imagine someone wearing a vest bomb walking into our compound. It wouldn't take much. Aside from my position, there is a short, winding driveway lined with hesco barriers, and another position at the end of it, but the guy who's sitting there can't see anything either. That's it, though. He's the only person between the city streets and me. I imagine someone climbing up the ladder to the rooftop where I sit. Sweat drips down my face underneath the mask, and coarse sand scrapes between the rubber and my neck when I move. Why wouldn't they attack right now? We are basically defenseless. They know this city better than we do, and they know we can't see anything, that our weapons won't work, that we aren't used to sandstorms. They know exactly where we are. I have the same old sensation of being watched, even though I know this is impossible. If only I could radio the other positions. Maybe they've been attacked already. It's getting harder to breathe inside my mask, and I can tell that it's clogging because I keep breathing the same stale, recycled air. I stand up, but feel disoriented and can't remember which corner I was sitting in, the way you sometimes wake up after sleeping in a new place. I am completely lost in the sand, swallowed up by the swirling vortex of this storm. I dizzily grope around for the plywood and the sandbags, trying to figure out which walls are facing which direction, but I can't. Finally, I feel the gun on the ledge and grasp onto its familiar metal form, using it to re-orient myself. I feel along the butt stock, the trigger mechanism grip, the safety, the cocking handle, the feed tray cover, the linked rounds of ammo, the gas regulator, the carrying handle, the bipod, the barrel, and it gives me an odd sort of comfort. I take off my mask and, despite the sand, the night feels cool against my face, the way it always does after taking off one of these masks. I sit back down, laughing at my senseless paranoia, and block the sand while I light a cigarette. I can't breathe anyway, like the guys back in our dusty little room, so what difference does it make?

Maybe Sage was right, and this sand will never come out, that it's even in our bones. Maybe years from now I'll still be picking these grains out of my scalp in the shower and still be scraping it out from underneath my fingernails. I'll wake up crunching it between my teeth, wondering if it was all real, if this really happened, because is this really happening? On an outhouse wall at one of the bases, I saw the lyrics to "Row, Row, Row Your Boat" re-written among a mural of graffiti. It said:

> Drive, drive, drive your truck,
> Look out for IEDs.
> Warily, warily, warily, warily,
> War is but a dream.

And maybe this all really is just a dream. Everything will turn to dust eventually, anyway, even our memories and the memories of us, so maybe Sage was right to find comfort in just being part of everything else, like this sand. I imagine myself being slowly eroded away by the storm. I imagine everything around me, this entire city, being ground into a fine dust and blowing away into the desert sands that seem to stretch on forever.

Kyle Larkin was nominated for the 2015 Pushcart Prize for Fiction for his short story "Minarets," which was published in *The Blue Falcon Review: A Journal of Military Fiction*. He served with the U.S. Army infantry and was deployed to Iraq from 2004–2005. After serving, he graduated with honors from the University of Wisconsin–La Crosse, double majoring in Literature and Philosophy.

Jason Arment

Bottle Rockets and Bad Memories

Rico had heard rumors, but he never thought he'd see it happen. And it hadn't even looked like much—could have been an accident. But like hell it was an accident. Rico hugged the ground, hoping Kim wasn't going to turn on him.

"Kim!" Rico yelled. "Kim, what the fuck are you doing?"

"I–I don't know how it happened?!"

Rico pushed himself up far enough to see the shooting platform where Kim lay prone. A dark circle surrounded him; the cement soaked with his piss. The Range Instructor lay facedown in front of him. Kim had shot him in the back of the head. Rico didn't know why the Instructor had walked forward off the line, but it wasn't far enough to be an accident; Kim had aimed right and up at a near forty-five-degree angle. The Instructor's body lay at an oblique from the shooting platform, arms at his side, his head haloed by a dark grass.

"I didn't mean it," Kim said, his voice sounding strangely serene.

Seagulls from the nearby Pacific swooped down and started pecking at some trash—a Recruit's leftovers from lunch haphazardly hidden in a pack. Rico wasn't sure where they were geographically, and that seemed important now, especially since he'd just watched Kim murder the only Range Instructor he liked. Now Kim was saying weird shit about how he didn't mean it, as if this was a video game and everything would start over. But that wasn't possible, that much Rico new for sure. The Range Instructor wasn't going to see his family in New Orleans this coming Fourth of July like he'd been telling everyone. He'd never get to eat his mother's soul food again, or feel the heat of the swamps press in on him. He'd been a real nice guy, friendly with Recruits. Kim was a loose cannon, though, something the whole platoon had been saying since they'd found him wearing nothing but a standard issue green t-shirt screaming obscenities in the shower room at zero-dark-thirty one morning.

"Listen," Rico said. "It's probably a good idea that you unload your rifle and put it next to you with the bolt to the rear."

No one had ever briefed Platoon 3111 on SOPs for when a recruit had a psychotic break with reality and put a round in the back of a Marine's head. There was probably a reason for that—the Marine Corps didn't want to put the idea in Recruits' minds to have it blossom into fruition later with bullets, brains, and the smell of gunpowder.

"Where's your rifle?" Kim asked, still looking straight ahead, his weight on his elbows, rifle cradled in his arms while it pointed down range.

"My rifle?!" Rico shouted. "Kim, that doesn't fucking matter right now."

All through USMCRD boot camp, Marines were one with their rifles. It was the start of a life where being unarmed was no longer an option. But the range was the only place where rifles had any bite, and every platoon was shaken down for ammo by their Drill Instructors before they left the range to return to billeting. Rico had left his rifle on the shooting platform when he'd crouched down and dove off to the side farthest from Kim.

"What should I d-d-do," Kim said.

Kim always started to stutter when things got bad. Anytime a Drill Instructor would scream in his face, he'd stammer back his Y-Y-E-S-S-I-Rs so badly it got everyone laughing. DIs had started doing it just for fun. Rico felt shame now as he thought about he'd laughed as well, and he hadn't laughed to fit in, but because he'd genuinely thought it funny. He realized that boot camp had mind-fucked him siding against other Recruits, even though he'd been warned by a friend who'd been in the Corps, gone to Iraq, and come back changed. Rico had never really wanted to go to Iraq, although he would have. His Military Occupation Specialty was Water Purifier. It meant that he wouldn't have to deal with all the bullshit that went along with grunt life. Or, at least, that was the way it should have been. Now Rico realized what his friend had meant when he'd said, "Some things change you."

"W-W-W . . . SH-SH-SH. . ."

"He's fucking broken."

It was McFarlen. He'd been shooting to the left of Rico, the last platform before the berm that separated this range from the next. There was a tunnel running through the berm, Rico remembered. He'd seen a few Recruits from another Platoon goofing off in one, and they'd told him how the tunnels connected the ranges and the pits where the targets came up and down at the end of the range.

"Let's get the fuck out of here," Rico said to McFarlen as he ran past the Recruit still prone on his shooting platform.

Sirens started going off, with brief interludes of shouting from the sound system; the speakers hung from light poles in white clusters, their sounds echoing in a muted, hollow way. Rico vomited as soon as he made it into the tunnel, his body retching the little bit of lunch the Recruits had eaten as fast as they could when they arrived at the

Rifle Range. Some pulp from his orange, and pieces of bread and meat. McFarlen ran past down the tunnel as Rico collected himself. Rico wiped his mouth and glanced out the open hatch to see Kim starting to stand up from the prone on his shooting platform. Kim was what the Corps called a "fat body," so he was having trouble getting off the deck and holding onto his rifle at the same time.

Rico looked down the three hundred yards of tunnel to see light at the end. From the way the light kept flashing down the tunnel he could tell people were running down it toward McFarlen even though he couldn't see much besides McFarlen and the lights flashing off the tunnel's white walls. The two-hundred-yard line was a hell of a place to shoot someone in the back of the head; it was the farthest they could be from the Instructor's Duty Hut at the very start of the range. Not that it mattered for the poor guy lying face down in the grass. As Rico leaned back into the open hatch and checked on the situation with Kim and the now dead Instructor, he saw Kim make it to his feet and start walking toward the tunnel entrance.

Rico panicked, turned the opposite way McFarlen had gone, and sprinted. He knew he could reach the pits quickly if he hustled, and he also knew that Kim was a terrible shot. Maybe he wouldn't shoot at him or McFarlen, though. Kim wasn't going to lay down his rifle willingly. As Rico made it to the light at the end of the tunnel, he didn't stumble down some stairs into the pits, as he had so many years before. Instead, he stumbled out of his back door, onto his lawn. His oldest son was standing there looking at him, an empty glass Coke bottle in front of him with faint wisps of gray smoke twisting out of the top.

"Are you all right, Dad?" his son John asked him, a concerned look on his face.

"I, uh, you know," Rico said. He felt cold all over, as if he'd just jumped into an ice bath, but he was sweating profusely. "What are you doing?"

"You told me I could shoot the leftover bottle rockets from the Fourth of July," John said.

Rico nodded, wiping his clammy hands on his jeans. He had told John that. Rico looked around for a lawn chair, then sat down in one unsteadily.

"Dad, are you—"

"I'm all right," Rico cut John off. "Just keep shooting those damn things off. I want to watch."

The sunset, coloring the thin clouds oxblood while the rest of the sky settled into a more rusty color. John kept shooting off the bottle rockets, even though each time one of them popped Rico winced so badly it looked like he might jump from his seat. Several times John tried to stop, seeing his father in distress, but Rico made him continue. When the final fusillade signaled the end of the evening, it was dark. The stars above them twinkled brightly. John went out in the yard to collect the pieces of stick and paper leftover from the rockets. Rico got up and walked out to help. When he got close to John, his son asked him a question.

"What happened?" John asked. "What made you this way?"

Rico nodded, as if signaling the affirmative would answer the question. John couldn't see him nod, he realized, so he tried to say something, but every time he tried to speak he choked on his voice. Finally, after many false starts, they both stood staring at each other, only able to see each other's legs in the dim halo of light cast off from the flashlight's beam. Fireflies filled the air, their lights throbbing in the darkness. Overhead a shooting star briefly lit the night sky, before burning out as it fell far to the east.

"I'm broken," Rico said. "Not like a toy is broken, though. More like when some of the gears in a clock won't catch, or when the front wheel of a bicycle turns wobbly after hitting a curb."

They both stood silent for a moment, the sound of crickets and an owl at the far end of the property filling the space between them. The longer they stood there, the bigger the gulf grew, until finally Rico took a few steps forward and placed both hands on his son's shoulders.

"I love you. You know that, right?" he asked.

"Yeah, Dad, I know."

"Good."

They walked back toward the house together, leaving all the detritus to soak in the coming morning's dew. Rico pulled John close to him as they walked, glad that the rest of the family was at some movie that ran late.

"What were you thinking about when you came outside, Dad?" John asked when they got inside.

Rico answered as he poured himself a stiff drink.

"About a guy I used to know, a Sergeant from New Orleans. And another guy I worked with named Kim."

Rico used his finger to mix the bourbon in with the soda and ice.

"What happened to them?" John asked.

And as soon as he asked, he regretted it. His father wasn't well tonight, and when he got this way, Mother always said not to aggravate his condition with questions. But once something was done, it was always too late to take it back.

"Th-they, uh. I mean, they. You know, what happened is," Rico stopped stumbling through his words and took a long drink, nearly draining his glass, then made another. It wasn't until he was done that he spoke again, this time his words fortified and distorted by booze.

"They didn't make it. There was an accident, and neither of them made it."

Rico took another long drink, then went back outside to sit on the lawn in the dark with the fireflies. John knew better than to follow him; there were times when his father filled with vacancy, and what was left of him, the booze soaked through. John closed the door and padded quietly up to his bedroom. It wasn't until the rest of the family returned from the movies that his father staggered into the house to sit in front of the television and pretend everything was all right.

Jason Arment served in OIF as a USMC Machine Gunner. He's earned an MFA in creative nonfiction from VCFA. His work has appeared in *Narrative Magazine*; *Lunch Ticket*; *Chautauqua*; *Hippocampus*; *The Burrow Press Review* (Pushcart nomination); *Dirty Chai*; *Phoebe*; *Pithead Chapel*; *Brevity*; *War, Literature & the Arts*; *Gulf Coast*; and is forthcoming in *The Indianola Review*, *Zone 3*, and *The Florida Review*.

Caleb Nelson

90 Minutes

Medal of Honor recipient Ryan Pitts remembers his last defining day as a soldier.

Ryan Pitts embodies everything a veteran should be, in bearing and conversation. He has true combat stories, and his patriotism is infectious. "We are a team," he said in the spring of 2015. "It doesn't matter where you came from or what color your skin is, we are all here for the same reason. We're all Americans. I love that about this country. You could have been Nigerian yesterday, or Chinese, or Indian, you come to America, you want to be an American, guess what, today you're an American. I love that."

Sitting erect in his swivel chair, Pitts spoke firmly into the pop screen over his mic at the WUMB studios for an oral history project, now archived in UMass–Boston's Healey Library. Professor Erin Anderson organized a class exclusively for veterans, in which we interviewed five Medal of Honor recipients: three from Vietnam, one from Korea, and Ryan Pitts, who served two tours in Afghanistan. We mapped their stories into a 60-minute walk through South Boston. It starts with Pitts' story at the Massachusetts Fallen Heroes War Memorial, still under construction near the Institute of Contemporary Art. Using a smartphone, you can walk about three miles from there, past the Vietnam Memorial at the M Street Park, to Castle Island while listening to the stories we recorded on the Voice Map app.

Salita Daniels (Army), Casandra Najdul (Coast Guard), and I (Navy) interviewed Pitts. He wore his Medal of Honor from Afghanistan around his neck, on request, above the collar of his blue shirt, shook every hand firmly, and smiled for pictures. He spoke with us in a little studio in the basement of the Healey Library for an hour and forty minutes, thoughtfully answering all five pages of our questions. We had a celebratory lunch with the Veterans Center afterward, all quite patriotic.

We celebrate veterans in America, almost gleefully, with great emotion, twice a year in particular, on Armistice (Veteran's) Day and on Memorial Day. Veterans get free meals with our VA cards and so forth, and are lucky to be so vocally supported. Our government makes jobs for people to operate and maintain weaponry, and we sometimes we need weapons. People do attack us.

Memories of 9/11 inspired Ryan Pitts while he was fighting in Afghanistan. "Any time I would see those towers, or anything with that day, I never lost sight of that was why we were fighting."

He said he joined the military to do something meaningful: "I was 17 years old. I didn't know what I wanted to do with the rest of my life, and I felt like going to college and picking a major was making a decision that's going to set up the rest of my life . . . 9/11 had happened, and we were getting ready to go into Iraq, and I couldn't think of any better use of my time than to join." Pitts boarded a plane for the first time in his life on his flight to boot camp. After training, he flew to Italy, and then to Afghanistan, where he deployed twice as a Forward Observer.

He would have continued in the military, maybe gone on to Ranger school, but he was injured during a battle and medically discharged. Now he looks back fondly on his time in the service, claiming that he will never do anything as great. "You can't be told about it," he said. "You can't read about it. You can read all you want, watch all the movies you want, there's nothing that compares to going through it."

The fact may be off-putting, and transcribing some of his stories I felt (sometimes) jealous or inferior. There are certain things I can never know or experience, but while Pitts was speaking to us in that recording studio, an indescribable sense of kinship grew between the four of us. We each shared a memory or two, and continued in more relaxed conversation after we turned off the microphones. My time in the Navy was exciting and difficult in its own ways, and no moment in time is really replicable. The experience of being in a team is exciting. Having a common goal can feel great, and every team is unique.

On July 13, 2008, Sergeant Pitts and his team embarked on Operation "Rock Move." Their mission was to transfer everything that could move from Combat Outpost Bella to a new location on the outskirts of a village called Wanat. Toward the end of the deployment, insurgents attacked their base.

The initial onslaught wounded Pitts and six other paratroopers. Two were killed. Grenade shrapnel hit Pitts in both of his legs and in his left arm. For more than an hour after, Pitts continued to fight and defend his position with his teammates, while critically wounded. Pitts' toughness and determination under fire allowed U.S. forces to hold the observation post and turn the tide of the battle.

When Pitts recalled the gunfight that ultimately cut his military career short, he said that his team kept him alive and motivated. "We did everything together, and the guy to our left or right was more important than ourselves. That's what helped us carry the day.

"Specialist Sergio Abad, Corporal Jonathan Ayers, Corporal Jason Bogar, First Lieutenant Jonathan Brostrom, Corporal Jason Hovater, Sargent Israel Garcia, Corporal Matthew Phillips, Corporal Pruitt Rainey, and Corporal Gunnar Zwilling; I'm never going to forget those names. Those are the most important names, because the rest of us, we can tell stories. They can't.

"People call us heroes, and I think heroes are the people who don't come home. It was 90 minutes of my life. That's all. I was there for 90 minutes of my life, and there's nothing special about me, but I was a part of something special.

"We had a vehicle that had identified some people moving in the mountains, looked like they had weapons, and so we were preparing a fire mission. While we were doing that, heard a burst of machine-gun fire, sounded like it came from the North, and then after that it was just a volley of RPGs and hand grenades that came in, and just the whole valley erupted. You could taste the smoke, the RPGs, from them exploding, and it was very disorienting.

"I was wounded right off the bat. I took shrapnel to both legs and my left arm, couldn't use my legs. Phillips was killed shortly after the onset of the fight, and we knew that this is serious. We're taking casualties. This is a significant fight. They're not just coming to fire a few rounds and leave. They want to try and take us out. I'm looking around at all these guys who are fighting, and some of them are wounded. It was chaos, and they're not stopping.

"Hovater had been killed up there, and we were at a point in the battle where they were having to check guys for ammo. They needed ammo, so they were going to take it off the dead guys. Hovater was Denton's best friend. Denton searched his best friend Hovater for ammo, told him he loved him, and then turned around and went back to the fight. Then Denton got wounded, bones sticking out of his right hand. He's right-hand dominant. He's got a machine gun. He's got shrapnel in his back, in his leg, he still stands up. He switches hands, and he uses this hand with the shrapnel and the bone sticking out of it to hold up the weapon while he stands up and shoots back. I didn't do anything more heroic than that. I know Soans and Myer, there's a point in the battle. The gun trucks are being heavily targeted, and they can't reload from inside the turret, so they get up on the front of the vehicle, where they're a target on a heavily targeted vehicle, and reload the ammo. There was never, for any of us, the thought of we're going to give up. They initiated it. They gained fire superiority, but we fought back, and we continued to fight, and then that tide turned. We had more guys come up from our first platoon. Apachies started coming in. We were able to readjust and react. Courage isn't the absence of fear. It's being able to move forward in the face of it, and I think about Jason Hovater. He was brave, because he could say to our platoon, he's like, I'm scared; he's like, I don't want to die, on other patrols, but every time we'd go out there and every time we'd get shot at he'd be right there doing his job, and that meant something. It was more courageous that he could manage that fear, that he could still do what needed to be done; now that's courage.

"I think you gotta do everything for the people that you're with. When you put them first, and you're willing to make sacrifices, you're willing to die for them, they will do that for you, and that happened. Ayers stayed on a machine gun. He got hit in the helmet, and then got back on it, probably knowing it was going to kill him, and it did. Later Israel Garcia and Soans and Denton and Samaru came up to save me. Garcia ended up dying. It's my life for his. It will be reciprocated. So valor was everywhere.

"The OP was a little bit separate from the vehicle patrol base, and I remember them saying, hey, can you pop smoke, can somebody pop smoke up there, throw a smoke grenade to mark where you're at, not ever thinking that the aircraft's actually going to come land there. The aircraft did, landed on a terrace between us and the enemy, and the crew chiefs got off the helicopter. Those med evac guys were unbelievable that they came in and landed, and then the guys got off to help people get on, knowing that they might not get back on, and when the awards ceremony happened, I invited those guys because it was important. They were a part of the team. They helped save my life and some of my friends' lives. What they did was pretty incredible.

"So they read the narration, and it's like I'm reliving it. The Gold Star families are sitting in front of me, and I'm just thinking about those guys that we didn't bring home, and how I wish that they could have been there. It represents the sacrifices of all service members, and it's a memorial to the guys, in that it's not mine, it's ours.

"We think civilian life is going to be easy. Civilian life isn't easy. It's just a different type of hard. Of the things that happened to us, they're very natural reactions to a very unnatural set of circumstances. I don't think that I'll ever be, I don't know, I'll never look at myself as transitioned. I will spend a lifetime transitioning, learning how to deal with what happened. Initially it was just that loss of those guys when I first got back. That was really hard for a long time. Even just the award. I didn't do anything more than anyone else that day. Right? It's hard to be recognized when we didn't bring nine guys home. Eight of them were at my position. That's eight guys I felt like I lost, but then, it changes. You deal with that, and then it's I miss the military. I miss that brotherhood. I miss that camaraderie, that family, and I'll always miss it, and I know, what's challenging is I'll probably never find it again, but that's also what makes it special. If I could roll right into another team and find something like that again, it wouldn't be special. I think I'll always be kind of dealing with that. I'm never going to be over that day, or what we lost or any of the guys that we lost, but you learn how to manage it, or you hope to. They don't have their life anymore. Right? They gave up all their tomorrows so we could have today. How would they want me to carry on? How would I want them to carry on, if I were gone? Life's meant to be lived, and enjoyed, and I'd want that for them, and I honestly believe they'd want that for me. So it's my job to be a good person, to have a wife and a family, and enjoy all the things that I'll get to experience with family, that those guys won't, but appreciate and know that when I get to greet my son when he comes home from daycare, and he runs up to me and gives me a hug, I have that because of them. They gave it up for me, and I kind of treasure that even more because I know that I was that close to not having it."

President Obama awarded Pitts the Medal of Honor on July 21, 2014, for his actions during the battle of Wanat. Looking back on his military experience, Pitts said if he had to do it all over, he would. "Being in the Army, I got so much more out of it than I gave, and I wish I could give more," he said. Now he enjoys a slower paced life, making a home with his wife, two-year-old son, and baby daughter.

Pitts kept a few small things to remember his time in the Army besides his medals: a wooden Punisher skull, the company mascot from their barracks in Afghanistan; a chewed up KIA bracelet that kept shrapnel from going into his wrist. Those were the more important things to him.

He said he'd probably give his Medal of Honor to his unit when he dies. "We're all just one team," he said. "It didn't matter what color your skin was or what religion you had. We had one mission, and that's all that mattered, and we were a team, and we were going to get there together, or we weren't going to get there at all. Maybe it's a little naive or idealistic, but I kind of hope that for our country, that we can all get there, maybe someday we'll realize that it doesn't matter where you came from or what brought you here, but we're all Americans, and we all want the same things. We want America to be great."

Caleb Nelson served in the Navy from 2004 to 2008 as an Aviation Electrician in an F/A-18E squadron. Since graduating with an MA in Creative Writing from UMass–Boston in 2015, he's been writing local news stories for the *Dorchester Reporter* and working on a poetry manuscript. His current blog is 39waystojihad.com.

Casey Titus

Interview: Preserving a Dying Legacy

1.) Who are you and what is your military connection?

My name is Stan Johnston. I have been married for almost 65 years, am a father of four children, a grandfather, and a great-grandfather. I am a World War II veteran, which was 72 years ago. I attended the Art Institute of Chicago as a young man. I am an artist, woodcarver, bagpiper, and a member of Gideons International, which devotes itself to distributing Bibles around the world. I entered the service July 19, 1944. I had just received my high school diploma, and three weeks later I got my draft papers to go into the Army. At that time, 88 percent were going into the Army and the other 12 percent were going into the navy. It was a time when our country was really "red, white, and blue." I had my basic training in Fort McClellen, Alabama, and afterwards had a "Delay in Route" and was allowed to spend ten days at home prior to being sent overseas to LeHarve, France, on a Liberty Ship. From LeHarve, France, we went on railroad boxcars, which were called the 40 & 8s for 40 men and 8 horses, then onto Luxenbourg, then to Belgium, and then into the Ardens Forest in the coldest winter ever recorded in Europe, where we dug into our foxholes for the Battle of the Bulge.

2.) What was the Battle of the Bulge during World War II and what was your role? Describe the scene.

The Battle of the Bulge was a German offensive that was made in December of 1944 and ended in January of 1945. It was the coldest winter on record. I couldn't tell you the temperature, but there was indeed lots of snow. Upon our arrival they took our overcoats and gas masks, and gave us jackets, canteens, ammunition belts, rifles, and "pick mattox" to dig the foxholes. The Lieutenant immediately told us, "I imagine you are all thinking you will be here for a couple of months, but do not expect that for we will be here for a couple of years." We were excited and eager to "get into the action" but didn't know what to expect. I was only 19 years of age at that time and a "dogface" in the U.S. Infantry.

We had two-man foxholes facing each other, so you had a 360 degree advantage of seeing what was coming all around. We were always on two-hour shifts. I couldn't tell you where the next foxhole was because it was so dark. We weren't there very long because we were

71

on the move. A lot of men lost their feet to frostbite or trench foot, where your feet get wet and then freeze before you lose your feet due to cut-off circulation if you don't keep your feet dry. That's why they gave us an extra pair of socks.

I was in the 87th Infantry called the "Golden Acorn Division" in the Third Army of General George Patton, and we received the Combat Infantry Badge, which gave us $10.00 a month more. I remember sending a letter to my mother asking her to send me a wool helmet for my face and wool socks and cookies, which I received six months later when I no longer needed them and the cookies were only powder.

The first week, the Lieutenant told me that the B.A.R. man had pneumonia and had to go to the hospital. Because I was a little bigger than most other men, I was instructed to take his place. B.A.R. stands for Browning Automatic Rifle, and along with this specific rifle, one had to carry an extra load of ammunition. It was heavy and needed to be carried with special suspenders, but the previous man had taken the suspenders with him, so I had to make a substitute with wire and rags. Without proper suspenders, the extra load cut into my shoulders and rode way down on my hips to the pelvic area.

I was on patrol with a young man named "Fishback." He was my age and I still remember him so well. He had just told me he "had a funny feeling about the day" and had just written a letter to his parents. We took four towns that day, and dusk was around the corner, when suddenly we saw three Tiger Royal Tanks that zeroed in on us with 88 guns.

Everyone headed for the ditch. I was near the First Sergeant, and he told me to leave the ditch, go up the hill, to inform him and make sure the Artillery Observer had called in the artillery to fire on the tanks, as the Sergeant could not see him from where he was. I ran only about 15 feet up the hill when I saw Fishback killed with the 88. He had taken my place only seconds earlier. I will never forget it! The tank guns opened fire on us.

Everyone took off for the woods. I remember hearing a family—probably a mother and her children—screaming. The unit circled back to town. It was tiny and empty, and we stayed in a basement of a house overnight. Our Lieutenant had a goal to capture a German tank and he planned a night patrol. Everyone had to ready themselves, clean their rifles, etc. There was not much light in that basement and it was difficult to see. While taking apart my rifle, somehow my BAR firing pin slipped and got lost. The lieutenant came back and he was so angry with me, I thought he was going to court-martial or shoot me. Needless to say, I didn't go on that patrol. The lieutenant was killed.

3.) What were your thoughts having dangerous encounters or frightening situations?

I think it's more than once that you think you're not going to get home or survive. It was a long time ago, but there are a lot of things that I remember, and so many times I could have died. The one guy that took my place, "Fishback," and the Tiger Royal Tanks were on us. At that time, God was never on my mind. I thought about my mother more than I thought about anything else. I think everybody had the same feeling, none of us knew what was going to happen, and that's just the way it was. All we could think of was survival.

4.) Do you remember the best moments you've experienced during your military service?

The best moments I think were when the war ended. My 87th had left me at the Rhine River, as I had severe dysentery and perhaps hip problems from the heavy BAR belt. I did not think I was going to make it. They expected a kitchen truck to come pick me up, but none came, so for days I lived in a cardboard box very close to the German lines with only one K-ration of food and one canteen of water. Somehow I gained enough strength to get to a road where I was fortunate to have an anti-aircraft truck pick me up and take me to a hospital. I had gone from 226 pounds to 140, pounds and all my military records were somehow lost during this time, so I received no mail from loved ones at home and only $10 a month until my records were finally found. It was a long time and they thought I was dead. I was in the hospital for about a month when the war ended. The hospital windows were all covered with blackout curtains in wooden frames, and they tossed out the blackout curtains like Frisbees. Everyone was celebrating. It was the end of the war and a great feeling.

5.) How did your family react to your joining and serving in the military?

They knew I didn't have a choice, because back then, once you reached the age of 18 you had to register for the draft. My brother, Dick, had gone in a year and a half or two years before I did and went to the Pacific. Both my mother and father had flags with blue stars in the window that signified two sons were in the service—my brother and me. And I think about my mother and dad and how they must have felt with their two sons in the service at the time of World War II.

6.) When did your military service end and why?

When World War II ended, I had only 16 to 22 points, and it took about 65 points to go home. I had 10 points for Combat Inventory Badge and 10 points for one bronze Battle Star. So I just had to wait. When I got out of the hospital, I was put into the military police for the duration of 20 months. By now I was overseas in the service for 2 years, 5 months, and 29 days after July 19, 1944.

When I finally got out, I had enough points to be discharged in the winter of '46. By the time we got out, they wanted everybody to join up as a reserve, but I had had enough. When I got discharged from the hospital, we were awarded ribbons for our service. They tried to award me with a Purple Heart and I said, "Wait a minute!" I wasn't wounded. I didn't feel I deserved a Purple Heart. My medals earned were Combat and Infantry Badge, European Theater, Battle of the Bulge, among others. I was present in Europe during the occupation time after the war and served as a MP in the military police in Belgium and Austria.

7.) What was the political atmosphere at the time of your military service?

Roosevelt was president at the time and was the only president to serve four terms before he died, and that's when Truman took his place. It was really a "red, white, and blue" atmosphere. Everyone was for victory. Everyone. There was no Democrat or Republican. Everyone was for winning the war and they knew we would win the war. It was just a different atmosphere than it is right now, because I look back on it now and think about my parents and what they went through. At the time we had rationing on most everything, but we were still a very patriotic country. It was a proud time to be an American.

Sixteen million went into the service at that time in the Pacific and European theaters. Over 400,000 were killed. I feel very fortunate I'm a survivor and God let me live. But now I'm just so grateful and thank God every day.

8.) Tell me about your life after your military service.

After my military service, I received a considerable amount of money. At the time, I wasn't very smart about it. I just blew it all away. I had never drank or smoked, but my life changed with the friends I was around. They drank and smoked, so I thought I had to be one of them if I didn't want to be left out. I pretty much got involved in drinking scotch. At one time, I was drinking two quarts of scotch a week besides the six-pack of beer I drank. All in all, I decided to finish some of my schooling. The war had changed my original plans so I entered a school in Chicago under the 9.1 Bill.

9.) Did you experience PTSD or other psychological distresses following the war and how did you cope with them?

I don't think I did. It was right after the war I went into the military police, and the transition was very smooth. When I did come home, I wasn't depressed. I didn't have any problems. At the time, I had no feelings about being a survivor. But now, I look back and know I was one of the lucky ones that survived. I do not suffer from any nightmares or bad memories. I think mainly it was because I've got Jesus Christ to lean on.

10.) Based on your war experiences, what advice would you give to men and women joining the military?

I would be proud of anyone who joined the military. I would hesitate to really recommend it today. I admire anyone that does join, but until every aspect of our government and military changes (I'm no hero or expert, and I'm proud of my service and what I've done), it's just a different world today in so many ways and I am concerned regarding the future of our military.

11.) Do you have any thoughts on the political and military climate of today, including the VA scandal?

Yes, it is very sad what they have done for the care of the veterans. Some of them waited so long for medical help, they died while waiting. Politically influenced people, motivated by greed or ignorance, have diminished the reputation and purpose originally intended for the VA. This is something that should be considered priority in our nation for the veterans of this country to be treated as real heroes for the sacrifices they have made.

12.) At 90 years of age, how can you reflect on your life, and what thoughts would you give to your family, friends, and the next generation of the country you fought for?

I have been very blessed, having a loving wife for almost 65 years and a wonderful family God has given me.

As for the next generation, I pray daily for our great country and hope our country returns to some of the values of the past, for I remember 70 years ago when you could leave your doors and windows unlocked and not worry about anyone breaking into your homes or lives. Today, you have to lock your homes, cars, etc., and have alarms, with all the crime reflected as well as the attitudes of our people. America was good in my day. I just pray for our country, the greatest country in the world and know today the best answer is the Lord Jesus Christ, finding a great church (like I have at Beacon Baptist and a wonderful pastor like Pastor Blalock), and praying for the return of the Godly direction and values our country was founded on and for its future.

I was privileged to go on this Honor Flight and was so appreciative of all the efforts and kindness I received on this trip that opened my eyes to these people still proud of our great country and the sacrifice the veterans had made. It has left footprints on my heart. I'll never forget this marvelous gift and the impression and influence it has left on my 90+ years. My grateful and heartfelt thanks go to all that made it possible.

Casey Titus is a 17-year-old resident of Jupiter, Florida, and attend Suncoast Community High School. She has always held a passion for writing and a sense of patriotism, and decided to combine the two. Casey's military connection to Stanley "Stan" Johnston was solidified after introducing him to Honor Flight in church. Stan Johnston and his family practically adopted her as a beloved granddaughter.

David Chrisinger

Interview with Major (R) Jonathan Silk

Major (R) Jonathan Silk: I joined the army, as I told my parents, so that I'd have a three-year break between high school and college. I became an officer after being in for fifteen years. I had this incredible training experience and wanted to become an officer because of that. And then—my combat experience—I was in Iraq and I got hurt over there. But then I recovered, went to Korea, came back, and then went to Afghanistan. In Afghanistan, I was an advisor. So we weren't out running, chasing Taliban, but I was in an Afghan camp as an advisor. I was the senior-ranking American officer in that camp . . . as a *captain*. Felt like I was more of a warlord or something

I don't know whether I was safer in Iraq or Afghanistan. In Iraq we'd go out and do our combat ops, and there's—you know, being in a firefight is exhilarating. It's freaky—you really feel alive. But at night, after our mission, we'd come back to an American base. In Afghanistan, I was in an Afghan camp secured by the Afghans. So we were advising the Afghan National Police, and then we're doing this training of the Afghan National Police trainees. So we were not doing combat operations, but we were there with Afghans all along, advising them, so I'd never know if I was safer in international combat ops in Iraq or in an Afghan camp secured by the Afghans, because, like Thursdays would be a half a day; they'd leave after lunch, and then they would go back 'cause Friday's their holy day. So Friday they'd go for their holy day back to their home villages. And then Saturday mornings was when we always had the problems. We'd call it, they'd come back all "jihad'd up."

David Chrisinger: **Let's back up for a second. So you were in the service for 15 years when 9/11 happened. Where were you when 9/11 happened?**

I was on an advisory—I was still enlisted—I was a senior enlisted advisor to the Louisiana National Guard, and besides Louisiana, I covered eight other states. So we were at this training conference in Austin, Texas, on 9/11, and after the first plane hit, a lady came running into the room and then turned on a TV, and we watched the second plane hit. I had read a lot on Al-Qaeda. Stuff like that interests me. And I was very aware of the U.S.S. Cole attack. I knew who Osama bin Laden was, that he had actually declared war on us—twice—before that. So I kind of knew that, when they said Al-Qaeda, I had background on that.

In September 2002, I went to Officer Candidate School. Everyone there had the impression that the war would end quickly. So after Officer Candidate School, you had Armor Officer training. When the invasion started for Iraq, I was there in Fort Knox, Kentucky, watching them make the announcement. When I got to Iraq, I got there in September 2003. The unit that I went to—I was a late deployer—they actually thought they were going home in three months. We figured out right after that we weren't.

Did you pay attention to any of the media coverage about the UN investigators who were trying to determine whether Saddam had weapons of mass destruction, and all the testifying before Congress? Was that on your radar, or was it something sort of in the periphery?

During Officer Candidate School, we had no real exposure to the news. We graduated in January, and General Powell testified, I think, in January. Sometime in early 2003, if my memory serves me. So I remember watching that, and I think General Powell's a great guy. A lot of respect for him. I remember thinking, "Wow, if he's up there saying this, then it's the real deal." Yeah, I have a lot of respect for him.

In 2003, I was stationed in Baghdad, and I was third squadron, second cavalry regiment, and initially we're doing a lot of convoy security. We did a lot of route reconnaissance. Those missions are typical for a cavalry unit. We started getting a lot more mortar attacks and rocket attacks, like in direct fire, fired from the distance. So we evolved into doing this counter-mortar, counter-rocket mission. We'd go out there—they'd get a point of origin on the radar. We'd go out and look, find things like the egg timer tied to the fuse. You'd find this stuff— you know, they just set it and ran, and so they were never in the area when they launched. We'd start doing a lot more traffic control points, trying to catch insurgents.

In the moment you're there, that is your environment, and it's incredibly dangerous but incredibly exhilarating when you're in combat. You engage something; something blows up. You're taking fire. You maneuver on somebody, call in a tank to take out a house you were taking fire from. Then there was no more fire. I got video of us, you know, cheering and laughing after a building with enemy fighters got taken out. And—which, interesting enough—we thought there was something wrong with.

We did a lot of our fighting at night, you know. So one day we had this huge fight during the day, and this bus pulled up about two hundred yards away from my gun truck, and, I mean, if it wasn't combat, it would be a comedy. This bus loaded with Mahdi militia men, armed, dismounting. I told my gunner to engage, and I mean it was freaking crazy. We saw what the weapon system did to the Mahdi, and after that fight, that day we got back to our base, and our gunner broke down. That was really the first time I saw, you know, what a bullet does, or what our weapon systems do. So I went and got the combat stress team. I think that's what we called them. They came over, but that's when we learned that laughter's okay. I don't know; it's just interesting.

You were wounded in April. Was that after you were supposed to leave?

Yes. I got hit on April 9. April 4 was when the rebellion started. We went into southern Iraq. My platoon, we escorted this one part of the brigade headquarters, when Najaf—we were outside Najaf, then we were in Najaf—we bounced around a lot. But I remember one night, it was like April 6 or the 7—no, April 6, in Najaf. We were getting mortared. We hadn't been told we'd been extended yet. One of my soldiers was like, "Hey, sir, I think we're going home on Sunday." I was like, "No, no we're about two hundred miles away from all our stuff." So after that, the Mahdi militia in the town of Al-Kut seized the town and pushed out the coalition forces. It was some Georgian and Ukrainian forces. They pushed them out—they were deployed without—with different rules of engagement than us, so they were purely defensive. It doesn't make any sense.

We got attached to this unit that was tasked to go seize the town. So in the town there's a coalition provisional authority at the time. It was the body that was running Iraq. The Mahdi militia, the Shi'a militia, talked about taking that building and getting control of most of the city. So we stayed on this coalition base, and we were with this heavy-armored task force. Now, they didn't know that there were three bridges—so the mission was to secure the coalition provisional authority compound—but there were three bridges that linked to that from the coalition base. They didn't know if those bridges would hold the armor, so we had Bradley fighting vehicles and M1 Abram tanks. So they did know that 20 miles north, about approximately, there was a bridge that would hold them. The overall plan was for our troop—since we were on trucks, we knew that the bridges would hold the weight—we would secure these bridges.

So our mission was to secure the bridges, and the armored task force would go north across that bridge and attack south. Intelligence told us there would be no enemy resistance on the bridges. We had three platoons—we had three bridges to seize, and then three platoons, and my platoon was the last platoon in order, but we had the hardest target. Our objective was the last bridge, bridge three, which connected across the river, and then right north of there was this coalition provisional authority building. So the first bridge went down no problem, no resistance. The second bridge, the platoon took it, met no resistance. Then there was an element of that platoon that moved ahead of us to clear the nearside of bridge three, the western side of the river. And there was a huge fight. By that point, you know—previously, as I mentioned, we had been told that there would be no enemy resistance—but at that point, we knew that intelligence was out the window.

So there was about a 30-minute fight on the nearside of the bridge three, and three guys from my platoon were wounded, and then they cleared that, and then we got an Apache gunship pushed down to us. We pushed them across the river. We kinda knew the enemies on the nearside probably had an early warning, you know, advanced element, reconnaissance element for the main force if it was out there. I had the Apache pilot fly around looking for the rest of the force, but he said he didn't see anything.

I had six gun trucks, and I pushed my first two trucks probably about 100 meters apart from us, from my element. I went in the middle, and then I had our rear trucks go, and pushed them across, and then I launched. And it was really—I was coming across the bridge— there's this little rise in the middle of the bridge, and coming across the other side of that rise is like going in. In the far intersection, there were these freaking waterfall tracers coming in from all sides. Because we were going to an intersection, and it was crazy. We moved into that intersection, like, one of my trucks is already smoking. They were taking rocket and grenade fire, and we were coming in that intersection, and we started taking fire. My driver, God bless him, swerved and avoided the incoming fire, the machine gun fire. We ran it into this big median for some reason Iraqi sidewalks are, like, five feet high. So we ended up hitting it, avoiding gunfire by smashing into this thing. As we're stationary, we started taking more fire. And as we hit, I got hurled. On the dashboard, there's this big metal GPS holder. I kind of got hurled into the dashboard. I had my body armor on, but it knocked the wind out of me. I remember my gunner was kind of out of it, but we were taking fire.

My driver wasn't hit. I dismounted at that time, once I recovered, and I'm moving toward the front—to the front of the hood, and I was going to take up a fire position and fire from the hood, and I remember seeing this, like, orange flame off to the right. And we got engaged with a rocket-propelled grenade, and it came in, as I was moving to the hood, hit about 15 feet in front of me. It did not detonate, or I wouldn't be here, but it kind of broke apart and part of the shrapnel hit me in the chest. So I was in the front of the truck—it was crazy. Front of the truck, and that kind of knocked me back, and I don't know how long it was I was lying there. And then my driver came back around my side. I remember him yelling, "Hey, sir! Sir!" And then as I kind of come in, like, getting my senses coming to me, and it's like, you know, "What the fuck?" And all the noise came back to me—like, we were taking a lot of fire.

I had some other soldiers there that were just hiding there, undercover. And I got them out, started rallying my soldiers, started forming a perimeter, started gauging the enemy positions. I actually took another hit to the side after another rocket-propelled grenade came in and blew up. I got hit with the shrapnel, but I had my vest on. And we start engaging and destroying enemy positions. So in that intersection, we're taking fire from the left and the north and the south, and then to the east. I had—about half of my platoon was wounded. Nine were wounded. I was number ten, but I had recovered. That's another story. I couldn't maneuver anymore; I didn't have enough force. So we just destroyed some of the positions, and then we ended up pulling back across the bridge, and they brought in another Spectre gunship that took out that—on the eastern part of the road, it ended up taking out that position. We ended up pulling back across and clearing out the rest of the intersection, then we linked up with that other unit.

Did you—did you know that night that you had, you know, literally dodged a bullet? That you had survived when maybe you shouldn't have, or did it take awhile to set in?

The next morning it set in. I had a huge bruise on my chest. When we got relieved—we finally got relieved, and my plate was cracked. I had big bruise on my chest, and that's when it really set in. They had some other rocket-propelled grenades. Some had detonated. I said I took some shrapnel aside from that, but other ones were coming in that weren't detonating. I'm alive due to poor Iraqi weapons training [chuckles]. I don't know if it was a dud or what. I don't know. I think about the fight every day—you know, daily at some point. After that day, I had about half of my platoon wounded. All of them came back eventually, though.

Did you guys know why the insurgents were fighting you? Was it just, they were—they didn't want occupation, or did they have some other motive? Was it jihad, or was it—?

It was more Iran. They were funded by the Iranians. We captured some Iranians, so we knew they were out there. And there were Iranian weapons being used. Later on, when I got attached to a tank company, once we went into Kufa. We went back to Kufa for a second time, and that's when we were actually fighting in the city. There was turret penetration to the M1s, from the RPGs being shot. Those were Al-Kut's Iranian forces fighting us. They had that type of weaponry, and they knew how to use it. I remember the night that turret was penetrated. No one was killed, but they, you know, the crew was wounded. It was crazy, hearing that come over the radio. Not very much will penetrate a tank. So we knew—right then, we knew there was a real professional force out there.

Was that like a "What did we get ourselves into?" kind of moment? Or was that a "I guess the fight's coming to us, and we're going to have to deal with it"?

It was—yeah, it was just like, you know, this is what's out there, we gotta go deal with it. And the second time we were at Kufa, it was just, night after night we were going down there. It was supported— we'd go into these support-by-fire positions, and then support the tanks as they went across, but the Iraqi—the militia would just jump up on these buildings. I don't know if they thought they were invisible, but we could see them clear as day, and we gave them these huge fights, going back and forth, and we just ended up sweeping them off the roof. They didn't seem to learn, because they would, like, they would always jump up on roofs, they'd silhouette themselves. It was just....

When we were in Kufa at this point, our counter-insurgency was put on hold. It was intense—high-intensity. Like, the fights I'm describing, we're bringing in tanks. It was conventional combat; it was all combat. The fighting was very intense. I remember, on the day fight I described, the reason we went down during the day was—this was May 28, 2004. May 27, we got word that al-Sadr wanted a ceasefire. What they were afraid of was all the foreign fighters—'cause we had captured some Pakistanis and, like I said, some Iranians—were all gonna try and get out. So we set up all these positions to capture them, if they tried to exfiltrate. The next day, we got the order to go in and verify there was a ceasefire, and so we went in, like, six in the morning. Driving around, people were waving at us, the Iraqis that were out. I remember there was the call to prayer. Like I said, the interpretation later was, you know, if you fight, fight for Allah and you'll go to heaven. Right around that time—I can't remember if this was before or after—but we came upon this four-man Mahdi militia RPG team, and they were hiding behind this big concrete thing. My lead scout saw the silhouettes of the weapon, and we dismounted, and my lead team went in after him. They captured two right there, and the other two ran into this building. They went in to clear it. It was such a small room, they just ended up in hand-to-hand combat. They just beat the hell out of them.

So we ended up, you know, capturing them, and right after that the whole city opened up on us. It was a crazy fight, like a three-hour fight, where we're taking fire 360 degrees. We ran into a—I had to take over an Iraqi's house, and, you know, rounds sitting all over the place. We'd go in and start clearing a house, get up to the second floor, and this Iraqi man and his whole family were standing there in this big living room. And my soldiers, you know, were pretty amped up, and one of my NCOs is about to hurl them down. At that point I, you know, I told him to stop because I saw the wife and the kids, and they were very scared. I took a second, searched them, made sure they didn't have any weapons. We searched their living room, made sure they didn't have any weapons. I told the interpreter to tell them, "Hey, I'm taking over your house. We're going to the roof." I had to get to a key terrain to engage another position, but then we built like a big fort like you do when you're a kid, out of the couch and pillows [laughs]. We secured the family, and so went up to the top of the roof. I identified enemy positions, and that's where I led the fight from. I was calling in tanks and stuff, and then at one point my soldiers ran downstairs to get more ammunition from one of our trucks. Come back up, and the Iraqi man came out—he was so grateful to us, he had made—the rounds hanging all over the place, he had made us Iraqi bread, pita bread, and tea. In the middle of this huge fight, and it was just really weird.

At any point, did you see the mission as protecting civilians from the insurgents, or was it more, like, engaging, destroying, you know, making sure your guys get out safe?

In that one, I mean, I knew noncombatants, they were the—the people were the prize, for lack of a better term. I always had that at the back of my mind, but that's hard to stay focused on, especially when you're in the middle of a fight. But in that instance, I was able to, you know, realize, take a step back. I could easily let my soldiers—they were basically looking at me for guidance on where to go. They were ready to zip-tie this whole family, treat them like they're combatants. I was able to take a step back and realize, hey, this family was just in the wrong place at the wrong time. That same day, we were clearing out—we were taking fire from this other house across the street, we were clearing that house. We had hand grenades, you know, and we were clearing out behind walls and stuff with them. If we were taking fire, we threw a grenade.

So we go in this one house, in the courtyard, and cleared that—threw two grenades into the courtyard, cleared that. Moved up to the front door, threw grenades in the front door. They detonated, cleared it. There was, like, in the hallway—the foyer, I guess you'd call it, there were three different rooms. The first two rooms, we threw grenades into. Cleared those. The last room, we were out of grenades, so we cleared by fire, but then, at that time—you know, once my soldiers went in there, under the bed they found this Iraqi mom and her two boys. Had we had hand grenades, we would have thrown them in there. We didn't. And that was like—I would never have been able to live with myself after that.

We got them out of there, and that was another example of where I was able to take a step back and say—'cause you gotta control your soldiers, your soldiers are so amped-up. And as an officer—or as a leader, it's not even because you're an officer, you have to be able to catch yourself. If you let it slip once, that's, you know, bad things happen. You can't bring your platoon back from that.

When things like the massacre or, you know, situations similar to that, do you think that was a failure of leadership, generally? Or how—because leadership doesn't usually have to face the judge at the end of the day in cases like that.

Yeah, I do think it's a failure of leadership. You're not out there with your soldiers—engaging your soldiers, checking on them, upholding discipline standards. Things like that matter and it keeps your soldiers focused. But I do think it's a failure in leadership. You know, when we took those prisoners that I described earlier—to secure them, I thought—the two of them in my truck, they were zip-tied in my truck. And my driver, I'd given him a 9mm. I came back to check on something, because they weren't in a secure position, and my driver has the 9-mil in the face of one of the—in one of our prisoners. Basically saying, "How do you *fucking* like it now?" He had the—like, right on the side of his head. And my gunner's up there, watching this, so immediately I know I got to defuse this, so I yelled at my gunner, I basically said, "What the fuck? Why are you letting him do this?" That defused it right away, and after that I had to move the two prisoners to another truck. But—I know I was a little more mature of an officer than others, but you have to always be out there to engage with your soldiers. Check on everything. The massacre at Haditha, I don't know how that—I don't know. I just—stuff like that is bad. I could see how it could easily happen. You let something slip one time as a leader, and it's hard to come back from that.

You didn't go into this earlier, but the RPG round actually ruptured a valve in your heart. And you told me before you had, what was it, 60 percent blood loss or something? Where it was only pumping 40 percent of your blood through your veins, or something like that.

Yeah, so what was happening was I took the hit. A very similar thing to traumatic brain injury—the impact, the concussion is what tore my valve. It's called mitral valve prolapse, so the valve is my fist, and the thumb's a valve. The valve opens every time the heart pumps, and this was ruptured, so 60 percent of—every time the heart would pump, 60% percent of the blood would rise, and 40 percent would not, would remain in the chamber. So in hindsight I had all the symptoms. But after that—you know, the next morning I had the bruise on my chest, thought I was good, had all my arms and my legs. But I was smoked all the time. Like I told you, after that day we're in regular contact, doing continuous operations, so I just attributed how fatigued I was to that. It was really from the injury, and so I finished out the deployment. I was really very fortunate, because, once again, got home and was having a lot of problems running and stuff. Once we got back off leave, and we started doing physical training, I was—my level of fitness was not improving at the same rate as my platoon. And, being a former infantryman, I was like, "What is wrong with me?"

I also had a lot of ringing in my ears from, you know, various fire fights. Went in to get my hearing checked because of the ringing, and they ordered a brain MRI, because a brain tumor can actually cause your ears to ring as well. I didn't have a brain tumor, but they found a small clot in my brain, so I basically could've had a stroke. Ended up at a cardiologist, who did an ECHO on my heart. He asked, "Did you take any trauma to the chest in Iraq?" I said yes, told him the story. So the clog had, some point after I'd gotten hit, broken loose from the injury, and I—I didn't really have any symptoms of it, but, I mean, that's how fortunate and how blessed I was after that. I could've easily had a stroke and been stroked out somewhere over there from that.

So that's when it was diagnosed. They said I was gonna have surgery—I had surgery. I really thought my career was over after that, like, I'm screwed. By the time I had surgery and stuff, recovered, I was still a lieutenant, and, you know, they were telling me, "You'll get a great pension disability." And I was like, "I don't need that. I want to stay in." So, anyway, I recovered, was able to stay in active duty. One thing that benefitted me is, the medical team on the surgery went through the rib cage. They didn't cut my sternum; they went through my ribcage.

Is it a faster recovery that way?

Yes, and also, for staying in active duty, if they cut your chest here [motions to sternum], you gotta treat that like a broken bone for the rest of your life. I couldn't wear—like, in Afghanistan, I had to wear my vest, but with that kind of injury—you know, with the bone, sternum, weakened like that, I couldn't wear body armor. So going through my ribcage, they were able to do the surgery. They never had to crack my chest open.

I can honestly look you in the face and say, "David, I pretty much accomplished everything I came in the army to do. I feel complete." But I wanted to build off something, 'cause going back to Afghanistan, my wife—no one will ever—you might understand this. So, after I recovered, got retained on active duty, out of the captain's leadership course, found out I was going to Korea. And I wanted to go back to Iraq, but I couldn't get out of that, so I was back in Korea, commanding—I wanted to go back to combat, in a combat zone. I didn't think I was gonna get my chance. But then we came back home and got deployed to Afghanistan—me being able to return to combat was, like, mentally was—you know, it helped deal with the injury mentally. Like, okay, now I'm good enough to deploy back. I was in an advisory role, where I wasn't really out chasing Taliban. To me, that was really—it really helped a lot, mentally. I felt complete after that.

David Chrisinger is an Associate Lecturer at the University of Wisconsin–Stevens Point, where he teaches a student-veteran reintegration course. He is also the editor of a collection of essays written by student veterans titled *See Me for Who I Am*. He is the son of a Vietnam-era Army veteran and the grandson of an Army veteran who fought in the Battle of Okinawa during the Second World War.

Essays

Carl T. Yates

A Case of Sodas and 5 Dinks

They say that truth can be stranger than fiction, especially in a war zone where the weird, the funny, and the scary tend to get all mixed up. The event I am about to describe happened to us around Christmas time in 1970, when our company was working in what was normally for us, a very quiet part of Vietnam. This time we were about six klicks from Firebase LZ Liz and no doubt less than that from one of the many villages in the area. Next to this military instillation was another little hill containing the land radar that overlooked and helped to protect the mostly flat area that we were given to patrol. This equipment watched for any enemy movement on the ground, giving our units excellent warning before any large build up of enemy forces could assemble for an attack against our outlying ground forces or the base itself. All the Army units that worked in this area were kept track of, and their locations were always known. So it was a given that anybody else wandering about at night had to be on the unfriendly side of this conflict.

I ended up staying in the 1st Platoon of Charlie Company my whole tour and had 4 months in country already. Therefore, I basically had my daily routine down pat. Getting up in the morning was time to get something to eat, of course, but then we just milled around for most of the day writing letters, playing cards, or taking care of our personal stuff and equipment. One of our three squads would be sent out on patrol in order to look over our surrounding area more carefully during the day, because the land radar could not identify everything that was out there. This same patrol/squad would often be the one that picked out the next bivouac location for that night. When we were moving our position frequently, and when we stayed in a different location almost every night, the Viet Cong had a very difficult task finding us, if they wanted to hit us with grenades or set booby traps in our path. Those explosive devises hidden somewhere near or on the ground were our biggest worry and came in a variety of shapes and sizes, like the IED's (Improvised Explosive Devices) our boys have to deal with in Afghanistan today.

Because the area that our platoon was given to patrol was flat and wide, a slightly elevated location could give us very good visibility over quite a distance. As we got closer to the hills, from a higher level most of the land looked like unused pastures made up of almost square or rectangular patches, on flat slightly rolling ground, interspersed with a few rice paddies. All around the edges of every rice paddy that we saw, and the other fields that were there, were borders made up of brush and small trees making hedge rows. Some of these were small and easily traversed while others were thick and tough to get through. Running through this part of the coastal plain was a tributary of the Song Tra Cau called the Song Tra. It was a small river or some might say a very large creek. This time of the year it happened to have a large volume of water running through it. Off in the west at a distance were more brushy hillsides that soon turned into the famous jungle of South Vietnam. To the east/northeast was our Firebase LZ Liz, the land radar installation, Highway 1, and eventually the South China Sea.

From one or more of the villages, to wherever our platoon was located in that area, came some of the local kids every day. How they found us so easily remains a mystery to me, yet there they were, every morning about 10:00 or so. We were glad too, because they would bring us a case of Coke and a block of ice to cool it with. We rubbed and rolled the cans of pop on top of the block of ice because the ice made in Vietnam was unhealthy to consume in the usual way. We all gladly paid the exorbitant price of 50 cents a can (15 cents a can back at the Post Exchange) for a little cold refreshment and a reminder of something from home. Afterwards, they would hang around camp with us all day playing cards and waiting for one or more of us to give them some of our C-rations. Or we might give them something we had gotten from home in a "care package." I used to have my mother send me those Fizzees, which were kind of like a Kool-Aid flavored Alka-Seltzer tablet. I sometimes put them into my canteen in order to have something different to drink. They were supposed to be a soda pop substitute and they came in a variety of flavors that tasted fairly good. I would break them into very small portions and try to get one of the kids to put a bit of it in their mouth. When I could talk one of them into it, I would gently place the broken piece on the end of their wet and outstretched tongue. Surprised, their eyes would enlarge at once as their mouth flew open even wider. The other kids and I would get a good laugh out of their various reactions, and I would try to get one of the other ones, who hadn't tried it before, to do it also. On occasion our medic would need to doctor their sores, because they would get these very large infectious ones on their limbs that we called "Jungle Rot." We genuinely cared about these kids, enjoyed having them about, and wished that we could do more to help them out.

One day we decided to take the kids along and go swimming. As crazy as that sounds, that's what we did, with permission of course. A couple of air mattresses were found and then fully inflated. We walked a klick or two to the Song Tra, checked the area out, and put our guards on the lookout for possible trouble. Although it was full of rapidly moving water that time of the year, the river was safe enough nevertheless. Jumping into this refreshing stream of water, we temporarily forgot ourselves. If I could describe it adequately, I would say that it felt like a Norman Rockwell moment. If it wasn't for our other concerns, we could have made a whole day of it. But at least the kids were feeling carefree, laughing, and having a great time of it for a little while before they returned to the village and we prepared to move out again.

One day they showed up without the usual sodas and we asked them what the problem was? They told us that across the river the Viet Cong had stopped them and had stolen their case of Coke. We didn't give it much thought until it happened again the next day. This was too much, and the irritation of the moment set us into motion determined to do something about it. At first, a few of us asked the Lieutenant if we could patrol the other side of the river in hopes of catching the enemy by surprise. Looking back on it now, it all just seems so *CRAZY*. The fact is that we were willing to risk our lives for a few sodas and to revenge the insults given to "our kids." I'm afraid we were that bored. After all, we hadn't seen any action for a while.

Mack was one of our squad leaders at the time, and he put the idea forward for the Lieutenant to consider. But the other side of the river was some other unit's responsibility. We might have ended up in a friendly fire situation, shooting at other US soldiers, so that was out of the question. However, we could do night patrols on our side if we really wanted to. Now usually, when a squad went out at night, they basically stayed in an ambush position, sitting and waiting on a trail for Charlie to walk into view before firing. We, on the other hand, had this wonderful notion of trying to walk around and look for the enemy in the dark. It became very evident, very quickly, that we were going to get ourselves killed this way because of our lack of noise discipline and inexperience. So we reverted to our usual method the next night of finding a good spot to sit and watch for the enemy.

Six of us went out to set up this ambush, and we took along a couple of LAW's (Light Antitank Weapons), illumination flares, a couple of M-203's (the M-16 with the grenade launcher underneath the barrel), as well as other personal weapons. Lying beside a sizable dike, we could lean over it to see what had once been a rice paddy, but now was dry and covered with short grass. We were fairly well protected there and able to see out in front of us for several meters. Mack however, started getting nervous, and the more he thought about it, the more nervous he got. Finally, he said that we all had to get out of there. But how? You can't just pack up and leave without having a good explanation to give to your superiors. He was nervous, but he seriously felt that he couldn't just pack up and leave. He had to come up with something plausible and quickly. Something that would justify immediately going back to where the rest of the platoon was bivouacked. After several anxious moments, he hit upon what he considered was a believable scenario as a solution.

"We'll fire up the area, call in on the radio, and say that we saw five Dinks," he said. "Everyone get it? We saw five Dinks!" Mack was more than ready to get the heck out of there. He told us the rest of the plan excitedly, "We'll set off the flares first, then fire the LAWs, shoot the place up, and then get the hell out of Dodge."

"One, two, go!" he said. Wow, did we ever! We fired the place up and then grabbed what we had and hit the trail back to the platoon CP. Mack reported in on the radio what we had done, while continuing to lead us down the trail as quickly as possible. But to his chagrin, the Company Commander got very interested in our little operation, called us on the radio, and wanted to know everything that was happening.

"We saw five Dinks, fired the place up, and now are heading back," Mack told him.

"No, stay there, look the place over, get a body count. I'm sending in some artillery flares overhead, so that you can search the place," was the Captain's emphatic response.

Everything had suddenly changed when that order came in, because it was exactly the opposite of what our intentions had been. It would be like going back under a spotlight on a theater stage and taking bows with us guys out in the open like that. However unpleasant, orders are orders. We did it, but with a lot of grumbling and cursing, quickly crossing then re-crossing the rice paddy the way we came, under the light of those large artillery flares. As soon as we were finished and Mack reported in again, we were on the move. We were told to quickly get at least 500 meters away because the CO was going to send in the big stuff. When those heavy 155mm artillery rounds began to violently shake the ground, we could only imagine what terrible consequences it would have been for anybody who might have been under that barrage. Only, nobody was really supposed to have been there.

After several minutes of hurrying back down the trail, we were almost to our platoon CP/bivouac when another message came in over the radio. This time it was from the land radar base next to LZ Liz. It was a report of 5 Dinks headed right towards their base and coming right from the area where we had just been.

Mack turned to me immediately and said, "See, what did I tell you? Five Dinks." I could only laugh and be puzzled at the weirdest of coincidences.

We were there. They were there too. They were somewhere close enough to become involved in our little charade turned into an artillery barrage, and yet we didn't run directly into each other. The next day a patrol went out to look the place over and found Viet Cong sandals under some trees not that many yards from where we had been sitting next to the rice paddy dike. They must have left them in their mad scramble to get out from under our fire, the artillery bombardment which had followed, or possibly both. Who knows?

Needless to say, that ended our desire for any more unnecessary combat patrols. We left the area soon after that, and when we came back later, there were no more incidents of the Viet Cong stealing sodas from "our kids." I have often thought about that night and those kids as well, and would like to know how they got along after we left. Maybe someday I'll get a chance to see that part of the world again, but this time on friendlier terms.

When I came out of the field for the last time, they sent me to various places on the base at Chu Lai in order to begin the process of returning to the states. I was to pick up my files, such as my finance records, dental, medical, and personnel files. There were also some last minute orders to retrieve, like my orders for my Flight and Bronze Star medals. As a matter of fact, I believe that everyone who had spent a year there received a Bronze Star. Even though most of us in my unit were proud of having done our duty, we did not take the medals we received too seriously. The one we fully recognized as having been earned and held by us in esteem the most was the CIB (Combat Infantry Badge). Wearing that medal meant that you had "been there and done that." In the process of going through the transfer, I had arranged for leave back home, and I received my reassignment for Fort Carson, Colorado, where I was to report a month later. At Chu Lai I walked or caught rides from one building to the next until all of these chores had been completed. I was mentally geared up to get on board that return flight and was contemplating what life was going to be like for me back home.

There were a lot of GIs like myself all going through the same thing, making it from place to place and trying to make sure nothing hindered their timely return stateside. Those of us who were scheduled to depart on the same day, and were successful in getting everything taken care of, arrived at the Chu Lai terminal ready to depart by C-130 to Cam Ranh Bay. I believe that it was there where we received a final briefing about what we might expect before we arrived at the civilian airports on the West Coast. The military personnel in charge at this transfer point informed us that we could be looked at differently than when we had left, due to the political situation back home. One of these bits of information we received included instructions about how we were to act in a less than friendly situation. The military was concerned about the possibility that we might be facing anti-war protestors waiting at the airport in order to accost us for our service in Vietnam. These protestors particularly didn't care for the America Division, we were told, because it was our unit that Lt. Calley had been in back in 1968. He was put on trial for his participation in the civilian killings in a place called My Lai.

The military brass, being politically sensitive as usual, sent instructions to inform us that we were expected not to retaliate, even if spit upon while we were walking the corridors of the terminal to pick up our baggage, etc. The room I was in was full of NCOs, and we just looked at each other with a sort of devilish grin. Our expressions could have been interpreted by any common bystander to mean: "You betcha! After spending a year risking our lives for our country, we will let some SOB of an anti-war protestor spit on us and just take it!" I cannot think of any orders that were ever given in the Army that would have been disobeyed more quickly than that one.

The next item of information to be disseminated to us concerned getting through customs as smoothly as possible. The concerns of the military included contraband and other items that should have been declared, that someone might have received or purchased on R&R while in one of those foreign ports. They also suggested that we would be wise not to have on our possession anything that might slow the process down by creating a situation that led to undue scrutiny. Hint, hint.

An example was given to us when one of the older NCOs asked, "Like what?"

"Like a roach clip," was the immediate reply.

"What's a roach clip?" he then asked.

The whole room burst into laughter because he asked that question. A roach clip was what held the last little bit of a marijuana joint, allowing the smoker to finish using as much of the drug as possible. The fact that this guy didn't know that was totally remarkable. Over there, roach clips in various sizes and shapes were all over the place. Potheads would beg, borrow, or steal a medic's pair of hemostatic forceps to use as a roach clip, because this particular medical instrument was one of the favorites. These forceps, designed to stop excessive bleeding, looked like a pair of scissors but were blunted on the end for gripping flesh or clasping onto small items. They also had a holding devise on the handles which snapped the jaws shut and held them together until pulled apart. This made them ideal for smoking pot rolled into cigarette paper, when the joint was almost consumed and all that was left was the butt. After that clarification about what would make clear sailing through stateside ports of entry in that final meeting, it was merely a matter of waiting for the plane.

Lifting off of the runway in the aircraft that would completely take me out of harm's way, I experienced the release of that last little bit of apprehension about making it through the war safely. We were finally going home. The first leg of the flight brought us to Okinawa, Japan. We then flew to Anchorage, Alaska, and from there back to the Travis Air Force base, from where I had departed one year ago. After getting through customs and released, I caught a jet for my final flight back to Oregon. I am not sure, but I believe that I landed in North Bend or possibly Eugene, Oregon. At least, I remember being met there by my mother and a mutual friend. The first thing my mother said, after I had greeted her and gave her a hug, was, "You smell funny."

My unusual odor was no doubt caused by the changes from living in a tropical environment for a year, and the newness of my uniform issued at Cam Ranh Bay. For myself of course, there had been a lot more changes going on than just my odor. For sure, nothing was really going to return to "normal" for me, or any of the rest of the men who I had served with in Vietnam. And, I didn't know it then, but it would be a long time before my life would come into some sort of focus and my soul would be at rest concerning who I was.

Carl T. Yates graduated in 1967 from Nestucca Union High School in Cloverdale, Oregon, and that next fall attended Northwest College in Kirkland, Washington. In 1969, his father passed away and he moved to Coos Bay, Oregon. In 1970, he joined the Army and did basic training at Ft. Lewis, Washington, before being sent to Vietnam and serving with the 1st Platoon of Charlie Company, 1st Battalion 20th Infantry in the 23rd Division from September 12, 1970, until September 11, 1971.

Casey Cromwell

Walking in My Dad's Sneakers: How Exercising Together Helped Me Know My Marine Dad

"My name is Annie and I'll be guiding you through your Beginners Yoga flow today. Let's begin in child's pose."

The mat hugs my knees as I kneel, curving my spine until my forehead touches rubber. I breathe deep and glance to my left. All I can see are tanned arms folded over a red mat, a Marine Corps tattoo peeking out from a blue tank top. Seeing my gaze, the man sticks out his tongue and grins. To others in the studio, he's just another class member. To me, he's my consistent exercise partner—and my dad.

The Center for Disease Control names several benefits of exercise, including controlling weight, strengthening bones and muscles, improving mental health, and increasing the chances of living longer. After years of regular exercise, I expected those benefits. The one I didn't? Exercise's impact on father-daughter bonding.

I always knew my father as a Marine. He joined before I was born, and, twenty years later, he's now a Colonel who still pulls on camouflage khakis every morning. By age eleven, I also knew that year-long deployments were part of the job—but that didn't make sharing Dad with Operation Iraqi Freedom any easier.

A few weeks before he left, I asked for soccer lessons. My dad played in college, and a soccer ball always sat in our screened-in porch.

"Just kick the ball against the wall and trap it when it bounces back," he said. "That's what I did as a kid. It helps with foot coordination." He demonstrated, synthetic leather slapping brick. "Also, practice dropping the ball above your knee and hitting it back up. Keep at it. Maybe someday you can do this."

Nearly every afternoon after my dad left, I escaped under the North Carolina trees with my soccer ball. As my knees burned red from hours of juggling, I remembered Dad's agility. When my foot accidentally shot the ball into the forest, I remembered his laugh. Hitting leather against brick, flesh, or even air acted as my therapy. And when I broke my latest record—40 juggles in a row!—I always sent him an email.

At the time, my parents and I never talked about my new obsession. My mom accepted that I'd often disappear down the block until supper; my dad replied to my soccer updates with smiley face emoticons. Years later, my mom reflects, "I was thinking that you missed him and felt a connection by learning to do something that he loved." As for my dad, he remembers being excited about sharing a hobby.

We do. Eight years after I learned to juggle, my dad and I play "soccer basketball" together, a game where we score baskets using anything but hands. When people ask how I learned this "secret talent," I laugh and credit my dad. I don't mention he taught and supported me from 6,399 miles away.

* * *

By the time I turned 19, in my mind, exercise and Dad went hand-in-hand. Sometimes literally, like the memory of my dad, sister, and me holding hands while finishing the Mud Run. In an hour, we survived five kilometers, several obstacles (including a rope climb, mud pit, and tunnels), and—the most challenging but rewarding part—each other.

When the starting whistle blew at 9 A.M., we knew our mission. Survive. Have fun. Finish in a reasonable time. But as we jogged past the halfway marker, our fitness differences became obvious. My dad was the aging Superman; and I, the past-injured athlete. My sister? She summed it up by screaming, "I usually only do this in videogames!" to one of the race volunteers.

After that, it became my dad's turn to yell—encouragement, that is. "You've gotta keep moving! Faster you go, faster it's over!" Whether due to Dad's DNA or his experience commanding hundreds of Marines, the Cromwell family is no place for sissies.

By the time we tracked muddy footprints across the finish line, we were exhausted and coated in grime. But we kept smiling, even while stripping our outer clothes and showering with dozens of strangers. As volunteers dressed as cowboys shot soap and hot water into the public shower, I laughed at the picture we made. We faced challenges and strange surprises—but we'd faced them as a team.

Relationship psychotherapist Dr. Jane Greer states, "When a couple works out together, the activity of exercise itself can physically and emotionally have a positive impact." In my experience, exercise has the same effect on fathers and daughters. The Mud Run proved that while my dad can be tough, he only wants to make us our best.

As Dad says, "Those who suffer together, grow 'swoll' together."

* * *

Annie's voice lifts above yoga students' ujjayi breathing and the soft beat of Beatles music. "Now, slowly rise up to standing, straightening one vertebrae at a time. Close your eyes and visualize your purpose for this session."

My purpose? I think. *Making sure Dad survives.* Before this morning, neither of us had stepped inside a yoga studio before. Intramural yoga at college taught me how to touch my toes, but Dad was more of a run-bike-cross-fit-or-die kind of guy. Then, at the start of summer, he suddenly added "try yoga" to our bucket list. I suppose old dogs (or, in this case, dads with dog tags) *can* come up with new tricks.

On our first day, we walked into the studio thirty minutes early, armed with two yoga mats and hand towels, two "Free Yoga for a Week" coupons, and varying levels of confidence.

"It shouldn't be that bad," I told him. "I have more experience, but you're stronger."

He is also sweatier, as it turns out. As we stand in tree pose—balanced on one leg with arms outstretched—I stare at our reflections in the mirrored wall. Me, a slim girl rooted firmly into her mat, fingers reaching for the ceiling. Him, slightly shaky and dripping with sweat. Not a Colonel and his obedient recruit—just a father and his daughter.

I see, for the first time, me teaching him.

* * *

When I first started working out with my dad, I didn't know what to expect. Magazines promise endless exercise benefits: a butt like Kim Kardashian's, the abs of a Victoria's Secret model, and an organic-loving, gluten-free vegan's dietary willpower. Beyond toning my body, though, exercise toned my understanding of Dad.

I juggled and realized that he would always be ready to catch me—no matter the distance. The Mud Run showed he gives tough love to trigger growth. In yoga class, I discovered that our teacher/student roles could switch. Exercise revealed that my dad and I, despite our differences, share the same drive to improve, stubbornness to overcome, and craving to learn.

My sister says she doesn't spot anything new in Dad when they exercise together—just reflections of his usual self. I suppose that's true. When working out with my dad, I don't see someone different. I just see a clearer picture of the supportive, determined, and adventurous man I call "Dad."

Casey Cromwell has published poetry, fiction, and creative nonfiction in PLNU's Literary Magazine, winning first place for creative nonfiction during her freshman and junior years. She also writes a successful blog (caseythecollegeceliac.blogspot. com) and has written for *Further Food, Beyond Celiac,* and *San Diego Writers, Ink.* She is currently a senior writing major at Point Loma Nazarene University, as well as the daughter of a colonel in the Marine Corps.

Coward Or Hero

The question of what one might do when face-to-face with death is a question that crosses every soldier's mind. Will I be a coward or a hero? It was during the Big War, WWII in the ETO (European Theater of Operations). I was a gunner-corporal with the 281st Field Artillery Battalion. On this particular occasion, we were billeted in two rather large buildings with a garage between. The buildings and the garage were built into a shallow hillside, which meant that although there were no doors in the rear, there was a row of windows high in the back wall, the bottoms of which outside were at ground level. The garage provided a most convenient spot for our mess truck, and the mess truck provided a most convenient spot for me as corporal of the guard and two other guards to pass the time. We came on at midnight, and it could not have been more than a half hour later that we heard a terrifying series of screams from one of the buildings. Within a minute or two, one of the guards, pointing to the windows in the rear wall called, "Corporal, look!" I turned to see the unmistakable silhouettes of rifle-bearing soldiers, crouched and moving toward the building from which we had just heard the screams. The guard then followed with a question I was not prepared for. He asked, "Do we shoot?" My immediate answer was, "Hell, no, we don't shoot! If we shoot, they shoot back!" All I could think now, as I stood facing the possibility that I could die, was that my luck had finally ran out. The question of hero or coward was moot. As it turned out, it may indeed have amounted to a bit of both heroism and cowardice. There is no question that the order not to shoot was given in my fear of being shot at and possibly killed. However, there was an unintended bit of heroism. Had we opened fire, we could have precipitated a disastrous friendly-fire incident, for the silhouettes we saw were our own troops from one building moving to the other building, thinking it must have been under attack. Had we fired, it's hard to guess how many of our own troops might have died. Such disasters were known to have occurred on other occasions.

For an explanation of what had happened, we have to go back to the previous afternoon when one of our jeep drivers encountered a German armored car and nearly lost his life. The jeep was destroyed, but he was able to crawl safely back to our lines. The screams we had heard that led us to what could have been a catastrophe of the first order came from the throat of that jeep driver in the midst of a nightmare, in which he was reliving the events of that afternoon.

So I, secretly harboring the knowledge that the order I gave not to shoot was motivated by abject fear, must admit that I accepted the gratitude of the entire battery for having prevented a catastrophe.

Hal O'Leary, now age 90, is a combat veteran of WWII, having served with the 281st FAB in Germany. He has been published in 18 different countries and lives by a quote from his son's play *Wine To Blood*, "I don't know if there is a Utopia, but I am certain that we must act as though there can be." Hal is a recent recipient of an Honorary Doctor of Humane Letters degree from West Liberty University, the same institution from which he became a college dropout some 60 years earlier. He currently resides in Wheeling, WV.

Jay Harden

Unboot Camp
An Imagined TED Talk

In 1945, British Field Marshall A.P. Wavell wrote: "It is a law of life which has yet to be broken that a nation can only earn the right to live soft by being prepared to die hard in defence of its living." His words speak of the contract between this country of ours and our combatants, something dear to me and important to you, more than you may know.

Today, I want to talk about the American combat veteran, what he and she needs and is not getting, something you and I, with one voice, can change to help them live soft after military service and help our country become greater in the process.

Imagine the past. A boy or girl grows up in the bosom of family, loved by mother, guided by father, chasing butterflies and climbing trees, enjoying the archetypal innocence, natural creativity, and personal freedom of American childhood. With love and loyalty, that child grows up to appreciate the peace and safety and individual expression that makes America unique. At early maturity, that child decides to join the armed forces and pay forward what was inherited on the shoulders of prior generations.

We all know someone like that child; it is a familiar story.

Then comes basic training and the reality of learning attack and defense in combat. This transformative experience is Boot Camp, a deceptive nickname for the deconstruction and reconstruction of crucial human emotions and behaviors.

The military must train you out of your innocence and into reliable action for your own survival and others. They do this by intentionally disconnecting you from your heart, your compassion, and your universal love of life. They replace these with honed aggression from primal survival instincts. Combat training focuses on death, the death of your enemy, to accomplish the assigned mission and preserve the lives of the good guys even at the loss of your own. America does this so well that our military now is the finest the world has ever seen. But there is a cost, a deep, personal, and individual cost that need not be permanent. Wives and mothers know this problem as intimately as the fraternity of combat veterans.

I spent 179 days in Southeast Asia from 1968 to 1969 and logged over 400 combat hours in a B-52D bomber. I accept personal responsibility for my share of wholesale death and destruction and for saving lives of friends on the ground. Since my time at war, some things have not changed for American servicemen and servicewomen, despite the superficial, patchwork transition services offered to today's veterans during and after discharge, but denied to us then.

When your killing and destruction are over for your country, you expect it to be over internally, and you expect to return to a reasonable version of your former life, wiser by the doing. This is an understandable expectation of everyone entering the armed services. This is the implicit contract between country and citizen turned soldier that we presumed. We took the risk of our own lives, of course, but none of us expected to be wounded again after service by our own government's disregard.

There are 18 other men like me in our weekly combat therapy group. After 45+ years, none of us have fully come home from Vietnam, stuck in the past to different degrees. This need not be. Our government has mastered the art and science of turning a teenager into a human killing machine. Our government needs to put a like effort into returning us to our previous state of humanity, as closely as possible. I'm talking about a military Unboot Camp while in uniform.

First, consider traditional Boot Camp. It specifically closes the open heart to bring out and unleash latent, uncivilized anger necessary to fight, kill, and survive in war. This training, later intensified by actual combat, endures unmitigated after military service and helps keep today's veterans sufferers, not just lucky survivors.

Aggression and anger are not natural states of being human. They can be transformed back to compassion and peace in people because these are our stronger inheritances. Untreated, military-trained anger and aggression add to the increasing fear I notice in America as a whole.

What, then, would Unboot Camp look like? My vision is based on my combat experience, the experience of my peers and current veterans, too, like my stepson who completed three combat deployments to Iraq. I want Unboot Camp graduates to clear the liabilities incurred from their combat past. I know this is possible based on my own successful and difficult personal journey of emotional and mental reprogramming to restore my humanity and calm my mind.

I started on this path in 1997, a path impossible for me without a guide. She, a brilliant counselor and an Army child of WWII, believed in my worth and never judged me or made me wrong. She supported my intuitive choice of tools and provided critical other ones. This lady understood the core of me that I did not recognize then, and cared about me anyway. Without a doubt, I am still alive today because of our defiant work together and what she mentored me to do by myself. I learned this: none of us can do this alone. Unboot Camp will, in effect, provide similar prevention tools to combat veterans, in place of the scary self-diagnosis and self-help I struggled through by myself after my discharge from military service.

Unboot Camp, in contrast to Boot Camp, restores the veteran by training him and her to neutralize that anger and aggression developed for combat, to identify and face any combat traumas, and to reopen the heart with a tailored combination of intensive, helpful therapies, such as art, psychodrama, dream re-scripting, occupational, music, movement, writing, cognitive, individual, and group therapy. Some of these are sometimes available within the VA health care system. I vouch for their separate efficacies because I have done all these things piecemeal. I can imagine their successful cumulative effect in an integrated effort during Unboot Camp.

In addition, I completed the New Warrior Training Adventure (offered by The ManKind Project), a weekend of masculine self-growth that follows the hero's rite of passage. I faced the dark night of my soul there and left with many treasures, including one I never had: a personal mission statement for the rest of my life. Next, I completed a similar weekend for combat veterans then called The Bamboo Bridge. Later, I completed New Warrior staff development and facilitator training courses. A few years after that, I learned meditation, breathing exercises, and other methods of yoga. All these experiences were useful tools in my restoration.

It's clear from my experiences that some pieces already exist to create an Unboot Camp that will meet the needs of all military members. Unboot Camp will also address that great residual fear of many combat veterans after return to civilian life, the fear of killing someone unintentionally, either yourself or others.

Terminology and intention are important here. Unboot Camp is not meant to be a therapy intervention that presumes injury. It is, instead, best described as skill training in changed behavior to frame a separate future out of uniform.

Unboot Camp has to be mandatory for all combat veterans, and optional for others, so no stigma is attached, and must be the last assignment in active duty military service. To be effective, Unboot Camp must match the mental and emotional energy and intensity of traditional Boot Camp. Unboot Camp must require each person to identify and address their individual service issues with the help of highly skilled facilitators in the healing professions. Unboot Camp will not end until an independent expert certifies your restoration or release for mandatory longer-term treatment after discharge. Unlike group Boot Camp, each restoration will be tailored to the need of each person.

I longed to return to my previous innocence after combat. It took me decades of inner work to realize how unwise was my intention to evolve backward instead of forward. Another measure of success in my imagined Unboot Camp is a forgiveness of self for the decisions of war that trades past innocence for a higher wisdom, with the possibility of continual change and growth into a better me.

Just consider Unboot Camp succeeding. Imagine the saved psyches, lives, and families, and the richness added to America's humanity. Then include the massive health care costs for veterans that will be avoided over each lifetime.

We need this Unboot Camp. This is fair and the right thing to do to complete America's contract with her veterans.

I anticipate the excuses: first—the Department of Defense and other parts of government, will say "that's not our assigned mission today"; second—the cost will be prohibitive. From where I stand, the cost versus added value to America is past debate. And if these obvious negatives are resolved, the trump alibi I expect to hear is, we don't know how to do it, anyway. The first two are a matter of public political will: you and you and you and me in one voice will make the changes happen. Don't tell veterans this can't be done just because it hasn't. There is no limit to what America can achieve, once decided. We always find a way through the unknown, even going to the moon.

As to the last objection, "how," I know from my experience some parts of a workable solution. There is a way out of hell beyond the after treatment of symptoms with prescription drugs or other desperate, self-medicating addictions.

To all who care about the welfare of America's combat sisters and brothers past and present for contributing to the preservation of our nation, I ask you, in the best tradition of American democracy: don't give up on us. In Vietnam, as in all our military conflicts, we didn't give up on you. We are worth saving.

I believe the start of Unboot Camp must originate in the civilian community where the great benefit falls, and that the solution appropriately belongs in the military community where the problem was born. To assure success, however, the responsibility for developing the essential elements of Unboot Camp requires a combined effort.

Combat veterans often return to the loneliest place in their world: home no longer recognized. No one today knows for sure the actual rate of veteran suicides in this country. A systematic, resolved solution still eludes us.

I want to leave you thinking about the idea of Unboot Camp with a poem I wrote seven years ago in my darkest days, called "*The Edge.*"

> I stood on the edge
> of
> an
> empty
> grave
> all tan and burnished brown,
> and heard the lure
> of deep, deep peace
> calling someone
> down.
> One
> of me
> responded,
> hungry to be reborn,
> to live today
> a different way
> without the scars and scorn.
> "Come back, little boy,
> beyond the blood,
> back from the rack
> of war."
> "I can't come back;
> the world has gone black,
> lost in the fighting for."

My hope here is to start a fire. My qualifications are my service record. What I offer is my time, my passion, and the personal lessons I have learned in and out of uniform. I think it is time to find out if there exists a critical mass of American concern and talent to help create Unboot Camp, a new innovation in military training so veterans can learn to live soft in civilian clothes, too.

And in case you are wondering, yes, I would serve again for this great land and all who live in it, eyeing the ultimate prize we all seek and the reason I served: peace, peace, always peace.

After eight years of active duty in the Air Force (including combat in Vietnam), then six years in the Missouri Air National Guard, Mr. Harden completed a career in the Department of Defense, then became a photographer and writer of short stories, poems, and lyrics about love, war, childhood, and personal growth with award-winning work in seven anthologies. He also has taught writing to veterans, but continues to learn from his secret mentors: five grandchildren.

Happy Valley

HM 3 R. Mosbaugh
Over looking Happy Valley.

Ronald C. Mosbaugh served in Vietnam with the First Marine Division, Second Battalion Hotel Company from 1966-1967 as a Field 8404 Corpsman. He also served several months during Operation Desert Storm/Desert Shield in Bahrain. He deals with PTSD on a daily basis and writing has helped him confront his demons. He says there is something about writing down his trauma, processing it, and talking about it—it is a healing mechanism. He was also published in *Proud to Be: Writing by American Warriors, Volume 4.* He retired after 31 years in the USNR as a Command Master Chief (E-9) In Joplin, MO.

Marilyn K. Smith

WWII Veterans Marched in Protest in 1946

"Bonus or Bust," said the signs held high September 28, 1946, on the Springfield Square. Police estimated the crowd at 10,000 persons, lined the square and streets along the caravan's route to the city limits. The veterans were headed to Jefferson City to make demands for payment of a $400 soldiers' bonus.

A family friend, Ressie Wallace, asked if I knew that my Uncle Murl led a protest march from Springfield to Jefferson City. I thought she meant the group of individuals walked that distance, which I found amazing. Of the numerous people I asked about the march, including my mother, Murl's sister, and Sharon, Murl's daughter, none of them knew any more than yes, they believed they remembered him leading a protest. Only while exchanging family photos with Sharon did the subject of the protest come up again. I was so pleased to learn that she ran across the newspaper articles while going through her father's things after his passing. Copying them for me would be no problem, she said.

We are losing World War II veterans at the rate of approximately 900 per day, according to 2011 statistics. Murl Eugene Owen, a former Marine who served in the Pacific, passed away February 1, 2009, at 92 years of age. Among his meager possessions, following his passing, were the September 28 and 29, 1946, *Springfield Leader and Press* newspaper clippings his daughter shared. They featured photos and coverage of the former GIs, whose mechanized bonus or bust march was lead by my uncle and Harvey W. Yost.

They were a cheerful, confident group of men before they left on their trek to Jefferson City, and Police Chief Walker called it "the most orderly crowd I've ever seen for a crowd of that size." Walker had posted extra police around the square—just in case. But he said he didn't have a single report of even a minor disturbance.

Mayor Carr offered a gift to Murl, if he "got them out of town without any trouble." When the caravan moved out of the square, Mayor Carr observed that "Owen has earned his gift."

I had to chuckle when I read the "Mayor Ponders What 'Present' to Give Owen," in the September 29 paper. "Owen called at his office one recent afternoon to discuss the march, the mayor recalled, and was warned that there must be no disorder. The ex-serviceman assured the mayor that none would occur, and I told him if he could handle it without any disorder I'd buy him a Cromo."

What is a Cromo? The article went on to explain, it is a brand of cigar which the mayor believed is now extinct. And the saying, "I'll buy you a Cromo," was once about as popular as today's "I'll buy you a cuppa coffee."

The mayor feared Murl didn't know the expression, just as the reporter questioning him about the "present" didn't know it. "Is the mayor going to come across?" the reporter asked. Mayor Carr frankly didn't know what to do about it. He was indeed pleased with the orderly behavior of Friday night's paraders, he said, so he might.

According to another reporter's tabulation, the caravan numbered 63 vehicles, including one school bus, and the vehicles carried 263 veterans. Later reports said the marchers' ranks were swelled considerably en route to the state capital. Included in the caravan were two "vets' canteens," loaded with sandwiches, candy bars, potato chips, etc.

The following caption appeared under one of the photos, "Wives and children will be left at home—just in case there's trouble. That was the decree of Murl E. Owen, leader of the bonus marchers—and his wife and daughter accepted his word, although they both wanted to make the trip to Jefferson City." In the picture, Murl signaled the caravan that he's ready to start, while his wife, Marie, and 5-year-old daughter, Sharon Jean, bid him goodbye.

Under a September 28 Jefferson City newspaper headline, "Governor Refuses to Act Now on Vets' Demand for a Bonus," Missouri's Governor Donnelly refused to consider their demand that he summon the state legislature to consider a $400 cash state bonus. "Owen, a veteran of Marine action in the Pacific and leader in the movement which last night produced a caravan of bonus marchers from southwest Missouri to invade the state capital, said that several hundred other bonus marchers were awaiting the governor's decision in a park outside the city."

Donnelly, speaking from the same landing on the stairs above the rotunda where he was inaugurated in January 1945, told the marchers that he was not opposed to a state bonus. However, he recommended that the former servicemen abandon their plan for the present and consult with their state senators and representatives.

Beneath him, squatting on the floor, were about 250 veterans, and the stair railings around the rotunda were crowded with that many more state employees watching the show. The governor spoke at an improvised rostrum while photographers snapped flashbulbs at the sides.

"Missouri bonus marchers booed Governor Donnelly today when

he told them he would not call a special session of the legislature to consider their demand for a $400 bonus for World War II service," The Associated Press reported September 28. "We don't have a form of government of threats or intimidation or of trying to stampede the governor into some proposition," Governor Donnelly said.

The former servicemen were urged by Murl to "stand as a unit for a bonus whether you are Democrats or Republicans and vote only for the legislators who favor it." He promised that the committee would send questionnaires to every candidate for the House and Senate, and would conduct an intensive campaign in each of the 114 counties for those who favor a bonus.

Comparing the procedure to methods used by Chambers of Commerce and the WCTU, he said, "If they can do it, veterans are entitled to the same procedure." Murl and Harvey Yost, co-chairman of the group, promised the veterans they would return to Jefferson City and "next time we'll have plenty to back it up."

Murl said he was disappointed by the governor's remarks. "Evidently he is not in favor of a bonus. He asks us to leave it up to the state legislature. He wants it presented in an orderly manner. If we haven't presented this in an orderly manner, I'll walk all the way home to Springfield."

As Murl talked, his listeners urged him to stay on in Jefferson City until they got what they wanted. "We're going to return to our homes," he declared. "But we'll come back."

The reception the marchers received in Jefferson City pleased Murl. He had high praise for the Jefferson City police and for state highway patrol officers encountered along the route.

Country people also welcomed the marchers all along the line, some even coming out in their pajamas, Murl said. In Jefferson City, some of the men were quartered in rooms previously reserved, and some slept in cars. A few were reported to have taken pup tents. Murl said one man had trouble with his car on the way to Jefferson City and suffered some delay. Repairs would come out of the marchers' funds.

Returning to Springfield Saturday afternoon, the marchers abandoned the convoy formation and came in small groups. A few planned on remaining another day in Jefferson City.

On September 29, United Press coverage stated that VFW Commander Smoot was highly elated over the conduct of the veterans who went from Springfield to Jefferson City to voice demands for a special legislature session. He was quoted as saying he would back the newly formed committee "not only in its bonus demands, but on all legislation that concerned the welfare of ex-servicemen in Missouri."

"Demands by Missouri's Ozarks veterans for immediate payment of a $400 soldiers' bonus and their subsequent 'march on the capital' here today," a September 28 Jefferson City news item stated, "focused national attention on the state bonus question everywhere in the nation. A survey by the Missouri legislative research committee reveals that the Missouri veterans of World War II do not stand alone in their agitation for grants from their state. Six other states in the union already have taken action, or action is pending on the problem.

"Cost of the bonuses to the taxpayers of those states range from $2,500,000 (or so) in Vermont, to an estimated $400,000,000 in New York. Some twenty states paid bonuses after World War I, reports William R. Neldon, director of the research committee. Missouri paid one, too, the cost of which was more than $13 million. Grants were made to soldiers on the basis of $1 for every day they spent in the armed forces.

"In Missouri, scene today of the first state bonus demonstration by veterans of World War II, the lower House of the Missouri legislature has defeated a move to pay the grants by raising sales taxes from two to four cents on the dollar. The veterans would get $10 a month for every month they spent in the armed forces, under the Missouri House plan. Money would be raised initially by a revenue bond issue, paid by the sales tax."

A copy of the petition that was presented to the Honorable Cliff Yelle, State Auditor—Legislative Building, Olympia, Washington, November 18, 1949—outlined the rules for receiving a bonus, such as "There shall be paid to each person who was on active Federal service as a member of the armed military or naval forces of the United States between the 7th day of December, 1941, and the 2nd day of September, 1945, the sum of ten dollars ($10) for each and every month or major fraction thereof of such duty performed within the continental limits of the United States, and fifteen dollars ($15) for each and every month or major fraction thereof of such duty performed outside the continental limits of the United States: In case of the death of any such person while in the service, an equal amount shall be paid to his surviving widow if not remarried at the time compensation is requested, or in case he left no widow and left children, then to his surviving children, or in the event he left no widow or children, then to his surviving parent or parents if actually dependent upon such deceased person for support."

A representative of the Missouri Veterans Commission researched the World War II bonus, and it was her finding that it was never enacted. Twelve or so other states, however, did pay a bonus, she said.

On my last visit to see my Uncle Murl, he showed me several medals he received only a few months prior to that time. They were presented to him by a veteran's organization, and he proudly displayed them on his bedside table.

A group of hungry veterans are shown gathered around the back of one of the canteen trucks. Murl Owen shown 4th from right.

Marilyn K. Smith's writing credits: *Buffalo Reflex* newspaper, *Springfield News-Leader*, *Ozarks Watch*, *Springfield!* magazine and others, plus she authored "A History of Highway 65, from the middle of the road." Her four uncles, Ray Thomas, Carl Thomas, Murl Eugene Owen and Wilmer Owen served in World War II. Her father-in-law, Merlin Smith, career Army, served in World War II and Korea. Her brother, Joe Wayne Thomas, also served in the Army.

Robert B. Robeson
A Memorable Medevac Mission and Moment

I've always believed that there are lessons to be learned from some of humanity's worst moments. War heads my own personal list. Armed conflict causes its participants to reflect on the jagged landscape of the human heart where trouble, fear, pain, bloodshed, and death are a dominant part of soldiers' daily existence.

One of these times occurred over 45 years ago in Southeast Asia during the Vietnam War. Hardly a day passes, since then, when one unforgettable medical evacuation mission doesn't force its way back through my long, stress-filled hallway of combat memories. It was a moment that renewed my courage and authenticated my emotional decision to become a medevac helicopter pilot.

From July 1969–July 1970, I was a U.S. Army captain and medical evacuation pilot in Da Nang, South Vietnam, assigned to the 236th Medical Detachment (Helicopter Ambulance). Life in this aviation realm was often unnerving. It was violent. It was bloody. It was deadly. In that one-year tour, I flew 987 medevac missions, evacuated over 2,500 patients, seven of my aircraft were shot up by enemy fire, and I was shot down twice. The seriousness of war became an intimate fact in a hurry.

The risks were always obvious in our role of evacuating wounded and dead from both sides of the action. We collected their ravaged, burned, and broken bodies from innumerable village, rice paddy, and jungle locations. Then we flew them to aid stations and hospitals or deposited their remains at the Graves Registration doorstep next to our field site battalion aid stations at Landing Zones Baldy and Hawk Hill, 25 and 32 miles south of Da Nang, respectively.

This type of flying—most often single ship ventures—was demanding. These missions were flown regardless of terrain, enemy action, and weather conditions, both day and night. A rapid response and en route care could mean the difference between life and death for allied troops, captured enemy soldiers, and Vietnamese civilians alike. Through it all, flying and foot-slogging varieties of soldiers built mutual faith, trust, and respect through dependence on one another for survival, encompassed by the devastation of combat. The ghosts and unforgettable memories from that conflict continue to rattle their chains in my psyche. This was especially true of one mission in early 1970 southwest of Landing Zone Hawk Hill in the infamous Hiep Duc Valley of I Corps.

It was mid-morning and an infantry company had just been

inserted by helicopter into an area about eight miles away. Two casualties had occurred, since the Americans had unknowingly landed in the middle of a Viet Cong battalion headquarters. One helicopter had been shot down by .51-caliber anti-aircraft fire. The long, white mission sheet I was handed by our radio-telephone operator (RTO) noted that a second .51-cal was also out there somewhere. Our ground troops weren't sure of its location. It said our patients would be located beside this downed bird and that's where they wanted us to land. This was never encouraging news for a medevac crew. A .51-cal round was capable of piercing just about anything, including our armored seats and Kevlar chest protectors.

A medevac pilot develops a "sixth sense" after flying hundreds of missions into similar situations. As we neared their eight-digit ground coordinate, my eyes began taking in the terrain around the landing area. A jungle-covered hill, jutting hundreds of feet high, was located to the west of the downed helicopter. If I'd been the enemy, I'd probably have put a .51-cal on that hilltop. If my hunch was correct, I knew our best opportunity for survival would be to fly under it and risk small arms fire over a broader area. An enemy gunner on this hill wouldn't be able to hit what he couldn't see.

My copilot identified the correct color of a smoke grenade the ground troops threw out to mark where their wounded were waiting. This smoke also showed us the wind direction. That's when I dumped the aircraft's nose and began a diving and twisting tactical approach from 2,000 feet toward the west side of this hill. We reached ground level in a flash, and I leveled off at 120 knots a few feet above a small stream that ran beneath this ridge and into the landing zone. Our Lycoming jet engine rumbled like thunder as we tore through the jungle.

I kept the body and skids of our bird below the level of the trees. Our rotor blades grazed the treetops on each side of the streambed. That's when circumstances took a drastic turn.

"We're taking fire!" our medic shouted, keying his mike switch behind me. "We're taking hits!"

We were committed, as far as I was concerned, and there would be no turning back. Enemy small arms fire continued to erupt on all sides as we barreled into a large clearing. I performed a "hot," 180-degree turn from 120 knots—that we constantly practiced to save precious time—and stopped at a three-foot hover pointed in the opposite direction.

I could hear both incoming enemy fire and outgoing covering fire.

A few seconds elapsed as four crouching infantrymen hurried toward us with their twin burdens of humanity.

"Get out of here, Six-Zero-Five!" the ground RTO shouted into my headset. "Incoming! Incoming!"

I heard and felt the "whoomp" of the first mortar round as it hit not far behind us. Then another hit in front of us. I didn't intend to hang around to see how this bracketing technique might culminate on a third attempt.

We managed to exit this landing zone with only a few holes in the helicopter to show for our effort, graphic reminders of the consequences of close combat.

At 2,000 feet, I gave the aircraft to my copilot and turned to check on our patients' injuries. Preoccupation with my own anxiety immediately disappeared because the sight of their physical misfortunes forced mine into insignificance.

Their blood was dripping onto the cargo deck. Our medic and crew chief were working to stanch the flow. Both wounded infantrymen appeared to be around nineteen years old. One had a sucking-chest wound. The other sat propped in a sitting position against the engine compartment bulkhead. His blue eyes were focused on mine and he appeared conscious, although he'd been wounded in the head by an AK-47 round.

"Sir, we gotta hurry," our medic said to me over the intercom.

I nodded but instinctively knew that no aircraft in existence could go fast enough to save him.

This blond-headed soldier's lips moved as he said something to our medic. Moments later, his eyes appeared focused on something above me that no one else could see. I'd lived this scene so many times before. He'd gone to a place too distant to come back from. His war was over.

I asked our medic what he'd said. His reply were words every medevac crew could ever hope to hear.

"Sir, he said, 'I knew you'd come and get me.'"

We had touched him briefly, but he, in turn, would touch me for the rest of my life. He died with a thanks on his lips. That final statement still haunts me to this day. What if no one had been able to evacuate him?

The following afternoon, this same ground unit called the aid station RTO at Hawk Hill and asked him to inform me that they'd found tripod marks from an enemy .51-cal on the hilltop above that landing zone. My split second decision to fly low-level beneath that prominent terrain feature may have saved us all.

Two of my dreams in life, from as early as I can remember, were to be a pilot and military officer. America provided me with those opportunities. We were trained to do what we did in Vietnam. My medevac comrades and I took risks every day in an attempt to preserve soldiers and civilians whose lives were often extinguished in war as quickly as the flame of a candle plunged into water. We were all in this deadly competition together, 'til death did us part, whether it was their time to go or ours. Sometimes there *were* moments when we were powerless to do anything about it . . . like this time.

Even though this young warrior's wound proved fatal, he was someone's son, brother, cousin, or boyfriend. It was our responsibility, on their behalf, to take risks in an effort to give him an opportunity of being reunited with them. Even on death's doorstep, he understood this and had faith that we weren't going to let him die alone.

His words and that mission have impacted my life. They motivated and assured me that I'd been placed in this critical position for a reason. People were counting on me and I couldn't let them down.

Over four and one-half decades later, and nineteen years as a medevac pilot on three continents, I haven't forgotten that young warrior or his untimely rendezvous with death. He has touched my life far more than I touched his. I will always be awed, motivated, and inspired by his courage and those final words.

Lieutenant Colonel Robeson flew 987 helicopter medevac missions in South Vietnam (1969–1970). He was operations officer and then promoted to commander of the 236th Medical Detachment (Helicopter Ambulance) in Da Nang. After his retirement from the U.S. Army, with over 27 years of service on three continents, he was a newspaper managing editor and columnist. His articles, short stories, and poems have been published over 870 times in 315 publications in 130 countries.

Armistice

I am leaving soon to attend my father's 90th birthday party. These days he is confused much of the time. A week ahead he gets the nurse's aid to call me, asking why I am not there when I have told him, just an hour earlier, that it is the following weekend. He has been sitting on a little bench outside the assisted living home since after breakfast, anxiously waiting.

Do not mistake this for one of those sappy stories about how my dad was my best friend who was always an inspiration. I never felt like his little princess. We were not pals. I don't remember cuddling on the sofa, cozy and safe next to my daddy. We called him *Father*, and he was not too warm and fuzzy. We were not a huggy, close-knit family that went to church on Sunday and said grace at every meal. He was one of the strict type, who always followed through on consequences for unacceptable behavior. Mostly, I kept quiet and watched. My older brother seemed driven to challenge his authority, reaping the *rewards* over and over again. I have milked my father's behavior towards us on many a therapist's couch through the years.

Sadly, my father could never hear well. There is a picture of him, young and slim, standing beside an Army tank during World War II. One day he was too close to the big gun when it fired, unexpectedly, and permanently blew away enough of his hearing that certain frequencies never returned. I can tell you that intimate conversations are not meant to be shouted. I have a soft voice, and it made a bad combination. When visiting him now, I have to speak so loudly I go home hoarse. Even then he often does not understand what I am saying.

Those of us who were alive during and after the war will understand how much it still influenced people's lives as a common reference point. For many it was still raw. My mother was a talker, and she wove stories of rationing and blackouts and working in an aircraft plant during the war. I knew that my father had not even seen my older brother until the little boy was nearly two years old.

We had no television and I do not think our 1950 Ford had a working radio. As we drove places, I remember singing the anthem's of all the branches of the military. "Anchors away my boys" and "When those caissons go rolling along" were words as familiar as those of nursery rhymes. A true patriot, she taught us songs of celebration, like "This is my country, grandest on earth," and "Oh beautiful for spacious skies."

She belted them out with such pride that, even today, I get goosebumps when I hear a reverent rendition of the "Star Spangled Banner." She had never been to war.

Father's khaki, woolen, Eisenhower jacket hung in the garage with the patches still attached. My brother and I would admire it. He was in the First Infantry Division. We knew he drove a tank. Army surplus stores fascinated us, filled with leftover items not used in the war. We loved to play among the canteens and mess kits and boxes we thought were for storing ammo. I remember sleeping under khaki-colored, woolen blankets that scratched under the chin but really cut the chill.

Besides the jacket and a dynamite set of binoculars, Father had other, more disturbing souvenirs. Most chilling were a full-sized Nazi flag with a huge, black swastika on a white field, a German pistol, and a 12-inch knife, engraved with something about Deutchland. My mother said the knives were issued, near the end of the war, to boys as young as twelve.

In spite of these grave reminders, my brother and I played war regularly. He liked to be Audie Murphy because this hero had won the Congressional Medal of Honor. I was usually the faithful nurse. On rare occasions I was allowed into combat.

My father never spoke directly about his war experiences. He did not join the VFW or return to school on the GI bill. He never attended reunions with his old outfit. I learned later that it was because so few of them were left. A tremendous number had died in combat. The remaining men did not want to reminsce about the *good old days*. My knowledge of war came from my mother and grandmother's stories. My grandfather, Boppa, was a "lifer" in the Marine Corp, who held nothing back when recalling his experiences in the Pacific. His language was astonishingly creative. Always prone to worry, I wondered how they managed their fears. Nobody ever mentioned a thing about that. It was a given that one did their duty. Bravery was not optional.

To us children, Father seemed grouchy and often annoyed by childish worries. We knew early to take uncomfortable feelings to mother because his answer was almost always to toughen up. There was no night light or climbing into bed with soothing parents after a scary dream. Luckily, I slept in a room with my older sister who, I naively thought, would protect me if the boogeyman appeared. Perhaps it was not the message intended, but I believed I was the only frightened person in my family and that it was safer to keep it to myself. The war remained background music in our lives.

My siblings and I went almost weekly to the matinee. WWII came back to life amid the bonbons and boxes of popcorn. Black and white newsreels played real scenes of Pearl Harbor burning or Yanks in jeeps being cheered by grateful civilians all through Europe. A bandaged GI was carried onto a ship by stretcher, smiling bravely into the camera. Some member of British royalty would christened a new battleship, smashing a bottle of champagne while everyone shouted joyfully and the announcer cheerily spoke of the ceremony. Today, parents would be appalled if Disney movies were sandwiches between images of the war in the Middle East.

One Saturday, the second feature was *The Diary of Ann Frank*. By then we had seen dozens of black and white war movies, but I still wonder what my mother was thinking. There were no "R" ratings in those days. It was a true story of a Jewish family forced to hide from the Nazis during the war. I believe they were hidden in the workplace of a Dutchman with inestimable kindness and fearlessness. The film left an indelible mark on me. There was no happy ending. My fears, on that day, found a real face to replace that vague boogeyman of childhood. This did not fit the war newsreel or the patriotic songs my mother sang. I left that theater stunned into silence and shared my fears with no one.

I became obsessed with thoughts about Germans marching into my town. Where would I hide? How would I handle such terror? Would I be brave? The only out of the way place I could come up with was to hide, with my brother, in the rafters of the garage and sneak out for food at night. I finally shared my fear with him and he agreed to the plan. Flimsy as it was, it was our best answer. Safety was an illusion.

The war slowly began to fade until Viet Nam spoiled the relative peace of the Cold War. It was in full swing when I was in high school. My peers boldly talked of how wrong the war was, how they would go to Canada or stay in school with deferments. I wanted badly to believe with their conviction that conscientious objection was the right thing. But Ann Frank and those Saturday afternoon newsreels kept me in an uncomfortable limbo. Maybe these boys had not seen the pictures of the liberation of Auschwitz with the black and white prison suits and skeletal bodies Had they missed the mass graves quickly covered with lye to control the stench of dead bodies?

I cringe, even today, remembering the evening my boyfriend felt the need to inform my father that he believed in his conscience he would never kill another and would go to Canada, if necessary, rather than go to war. In the stunned silence that followed, his remark seemed so childish to me. I felt shame for bringing this jerk home. This privileged boy might as well have slapped my father's face with his arrogance. My father, always a gentleman, was too polite to reply more than a brief rebuttal, but I knew he was furious. The teenager in me was mortified by my war-mongering father, afraid he would *go ape*. In my lack of maturity, I was afraid he looked like an ignorant hawk, a fool to this young man.

Now, I visit my father in his tiny apartment where he is a prisoner in his brown recliner, equipped to help him stand. It is an assisted living facility. Because of age and mellowness, he has chosen to open up his life for the first time. My mother's death had been the end of my controlled father. The fears held back 70 years spilled out. My John Wayne parent sat weeping with all the grief he had kept locked up for decades. So overwhelmed, he could not attended the funeral, he was given no choice. His doctor sent him to a psychiatrist who diagnosed him with Post Traumatic Stress Disorder. My father, man of steel, was prescribed an antidepressant and he took it.

The day he slipped that quietly into the conversation was a shocking realization for me. It was the missing puzzle piece that finally completed the picture, illuminated this stranger I'd spent a lifetime trying to decipher. For the first time, I felt compassion. He asked if I would go see the movie *Saving Private Ryan*. Soon after, I attended a matinee. Sitting there in the dark, tears leaking down my face for all I had misunderstood, I began to understand. My young father had landed on the beach at Omaha and was never, ever the same.

Like so many other elderly people, his short-term memory is shot. I must remind him who my children are and the city I live in. But he is able to tell us a little of the horrors of long years in Europe and how difficult it was to be a second Lieutenant in charge of men's lives when barely old enough to grow a full beard.

When given sleeping pills following the bad fall that made it impossible for him to remain living alone, he hallucinated and crawled on the floor frantically searching for dead and wounded. He hates the song "When Johnny Comes Marching Home," because so many did not have that honor.

My brother has gotten in touch with the VA. Father was surprised to learn he had been awarded a "Distinguished Combat Record." He had not received one but two purple hearts. He was shot twice, shot at countless times. He witnessed men blown to pieces while he sat a few feet away. Those years of sleeping in snow, eating C-rations, when lucky, and watching man after man die made his answer to close himself off seem rational.

I am sorry he had to wait so long, to be honest. I'd like to put a warm ending on this story, that we are great pals now and he is enjoying a wonderful old age. Visiting him in assisted living is sad, but also a blessing. Over this time, I have learned so much about his life that I would not have heard if we had only chatted at family parties. I have made peace with my childhood in that dark, hot room at Arcadia Place. I know, now, he has loved me all those years I doubted.

Sadly, because of the accident, he sits with white haired, deaf people and their walkers, remembering how it was. I cannot rescue him. Each time I drive away, my guts are knotted in grief for this quiet man. Nobody deserves to end up wearing diapers in such a dreary place.

He never complains. He misses my mother terribly but does not burden his children with guilt, always just seems happy to see us and sad when we have to leave. He has become something of a hero to me as he has faced such a loss of freedom with a stoicism I do not believe I could muster. Last time I saw him I asked how he was able to deal with all he faces in this sad dormitory. "It is all in controlling my mind," he answered. I guess he learned that trick hiding for days in a Belgium forest while Germans hunted him and his men so many years ago.

Susan Correa is a retired family therapist. She's had essays in the *Ventura Star* and Columbian newspapers. Her poetry has been published in *Rivertalk* and *Verve* magazines. Her father, a World War ll Army Veteran, finally opened up about his war experiences almost 70 years after the war in Europe ended. He was there from DDay until after VE Day. She wrote this to honor him for his sacrifice for our freedom.

Valerie E. Young

Future Hero

Valerie Elizabeth Young is a veteran of the United States Air Forces. She served approximately ten years, with a deployments in Iraq. She is mother to six-year-old son Sultan and five-year-old daughter VerTRUoz (pronounced Virtuous). She is a Head Start advocate and parent ambassador. Recently she was presented with a national parent of the year award at the Annual Head Start conference in Nashville.

Bobby & the Pole

Hector Luis Martinez—"Bobby" to his friends—private first class, paratrooper, 11th Pathfinder Company of the 11th Air Assault Division. The year was 1964, and as Roosevelt said 20 years before that, it was a year that would live in infamy . . . well, for me and my family anyway. Hector was 21 years old; he volunteered to join the army, he said, to give his only son a better life. Hector, or Bobby, was my father. I lost my mother that year to a car accident, and months later my father would suffer death through a means that I and my family had no real knowledge or understanding of. We know what we were told, but we didn't believe it.

Bobby married his high-school sweetheart—that's where I came into play. Back then, early 60s, segregation was king down South. I'm a Floridian, as South as you can get in the Union. They went to Blake High, in Tampa, where it didn't matter what culture you came from, if your skin color was darker than it should be, then you went to an all-Black school. That's just the way it was.

It would have been another normal life and story. Young couple in love, dashingly cute firstborn, they had a full future ahead of them. It was the early 60s, and America was going to soon experience a change it wasn't prepared for. President Kennedy would be gunned down at noon in Dallas by a loser loner, with hundreds witnessing the murder, the Beatles would soon invade the States and music would never be the same, Marilyn Monroe would be found dead in her bedroom by her housekeeper—the reasons still under debate—and the Civil Rights movement was about to blow wide open. America would never be the same.

Of course I would have no way of knowing, as a toddler, that my life would change forever too. As I was growing up, my grandparents idolized my father. I grew up knowing that my father had died in the Army and believed he died some mysterious heroic death; I hated the Army, yet respected the Army because my father gave his life. I truly adored my father.

"Your father was a good man, son," Pop, my grandfather, told me, "he loved his family, his country and his Creator." Bobby was the kid everyone was friends with, a talented singer, artist, and mechanic. He was very devoted to family and usually the life of the party. He imitated

Loony Tunes voices and was popular with the ladies. Music ran in the blood, so he was in a do wop group in high school and a singing group in the Army. I have pictures of all this in albums that I'd frequent countless times throughout my childhood. Instead of a father, I saw him as a big brother I never got to know, and everyone he touched loved him. So I grew up idolizing him myself. When I asked about the circumstances of his death, though, I was usually hushed and told not to dig up old bones. It wasn't until I was an adult, when I ruffled through some old military papers I found in a metal box in my grandparent's closet, that I found out. Private Hector Luis Martinez was electrocuted, fell off an electric pole, and plummeted 40 feet to near death. He lay in a military hospital a few days, lingering in pain and paralyzed. His parents went to see him, just before he passed away. He begged them to please raise me the way they raised him. I think they did a great job. But I just couldn't accept that—he fell off a pole? That's it? He wasn't even an electrician, what was he doing on a pole? Was the Army hiding something, was it Agent Orange? Was it a Manchurian Candidate espionage type thing? Was he a Rambo that got shot down by the enemy? I had to know.

Enter the *Information Age*. Actually I have to credit a friend of mine who told me, "Why don't you request information from the military? You're his son, they have to give it to you." I'm an I.T. guy, I work with information all day, and the thought had never occurred to me. So I did. Then I received the packet. I waited hours to open it; I don't know . . . nervousness, not really wanting to know? But I sat in my private study at home, opened the envelope and poured out the sheets of paper addressed to me. I smiled, I frowned, I got mad, I cried, I was dumbfounded. It was true. Bobby Martinez fell off of an electric pole. I put the papers down, dumbfounded. Then something hit me . . . there were two names that came up repeatedly on the papers. One was his partner, one was his commanding officer. I became obsessed, if I hear from one of them, then I'll know for sure.

I tried my best online and found one of them. The name of his commanding officer coincided with a man now serving in the military. I emailed him, explained who I was, and asked if he remembered the incident. Gotta love the internet, the man was the *son* of my father's commanding officer, he forwarded my mail to his father. Days later, sitting at work, I get an email from someone with the subject line "your father." The Colonel explained to me that he remembered vividly the incident and shed light to a fifty-plus-year-old mystery to me in two emails.

I asked him, did my father really fall off an electric pole? The following is his *word for word* reply.

"Your father Bobby was part of the Pathfinder unit. To understand what he was doing that night, I'll first tell you a little about Pathfinder units and their mission. Pathfinders are highly trained parachute-qualified infantrymen. Some are also Ranger qualified. All are hand-picked for their physical and mental toughness, ability to operate in small groups or alone, drive-on attitude, and willingness to do what it takes to accomplish the assigned mission. They are specially trained in recon and infiltration techniques, and setting up and controlling day and night helicopter landing zones, parachute drop zones, and airfields for assault transports. Their equipment includes lights and other visual signaling gear, radio homing beacons, tools to clear landing areas, and radios for aircraft control and contact with other ground units. The lineage of Pathfinder units dates back to the teams that led the airborne part of the Normandy invasion on D-Day, June 6, 1944.

"The 11th Air Assault Division was engaged in a series of tests over a two-year period in 1963–65 that were designed to test the Army's air mobility concept, which was just being developed at the time. We had many long field exercises in Georgia and North and South Carolina. The division had over 400 helicopters and fixed wing aircraft, and the 11th Pathfinder Company worked day and night to provide the support I described earlier. On the night he died, I recall he was part of a six-man Pathfinder team that had the mission of establishing a night landing zone in a farm field for a large group of helicopters. I don't remember whether they parachuted into the area or infiltrated over land. While some team members cleared obstacles in the field and set up radios and landing lights, your Dad and one other trooper had the job of putting red lights near the top of the poles of a small country power line running along a dirt road at the approach end of the field. This was not an easy task, especially at night, but these obstacle lights were critical because the helicopter formation had to pass directly over the power line at low altitude as they came in to land. Naturally, Pathfinders had to be very careful in performing this task, but they had been trained how to do it safely. I believe they had successfully climbed and marked several poles, but the trooper with your Dad was unable to place the light on one pole. Your Dad said he would do it for him, and in the process he accidentally came in contact with a hot line and was killed.

"The 11th Air Assault Division later became the 1st Cavalry Division and we deployed to Vietnam in August 1965 where 'The Cav' established an outstanding combat record in some of the toughest fighting of that war. Bobby would have gone with us. I had a lot of great troopers in the company, and your Dad was one of our finest young soldiers. I hope this has been helpful to you in getting a better understanding of your father's service, and the esteem and respect we had for him both as a soldier and as a person. I remember him as a fine young paratrooper, always willing to do whatever was necessary to accomplish the assigned mission. He was very well liked in the company, and his loss was a great shock to all of us. I and several of his fellow Pathfinders flew to Tampa to attend his funeral. This all happened a long time ago, but if I can be of further assistance, don't hesitate to ask."

As you can imagine, I was in tears by the end of that email. My father *was* Rambo. Ok, ok he wasn't Rambo, but he served in a group that did Rambo stuff. Not that it mattered to anyone else; I just really needed to know. I needed closure. But to hear the full story in detail just blew me away. So I get to share my excitement and closure with my son, Bobby's only grand-child, who has been curious about his ancestors. Now I can give him a full birth to death story of the man who lived only 21 years but shared a lifetime of joy, sorrow, and pride in my life. Bobby lives through my son and for generations to come.

Rod Martinez was born and raised in Tampa, Florida, and was attracted to words at an early age. He wrote his first book *The Boy Who Liked To Read* (about himself) with construction paper and pencil in the grade school on his own—wasn't a class assignment.

Government Girls

In 1941 we learned from the radio that the Japanese had bombed Pearl Harbor and President Roosevelt had declared war. Our sleepy little rural town, Lesterville, Missouri, came alive with activity as we struggled with gas and food rationing, and with many of our young men enlisting in military service. President Roosevelt issued a call for Government Girls to fill the jobs of young men going to war.

In May of 1942, right after school was out our sophomore year, Ruby Jean Lester and I headed for St. Louis to find summer work. I had just turned 16 in April, and Ruby Jean would not be 16 until fall. We were joined by Ruby Moses, 16, who had just completed her junior year at Lesterville High; she also had a fall birthday. Then a relative of Ruby Jean's family, Lucy Quertermous, a Charleston High graduate at 15 with a fall birthday, made up our group of four teenagers. So, two 15 year olds and two 16 year olds made the decision to answer the President's call and be a part of the War effort by signing up to become Government Girls. We were thinking we were going to be assigned to Hawaii, Panama Canal, or maybe Washington, D.C. At the last minute Ruby Moses decided to stay and finish her last year of school. The other girls obtained permission from their parents to make the trip, but I did not. And for a very good reason, I thought. My mother would just say no, and I couldn't bear the thought of missing out on this opportunity.

We received six weeks training at the Buder Building in St. Louis then signed a contract agreeing to stay at least a year in return for the Government to pay our train fare to and from wherever they decided to send us, which was Washington, D.C.. It was thought we were too young to be sent out of the country. Since Hawaii was our first choice, we were mildly disappointed but still excited to be accepted. We thought of ourselves as new recruits as we trained and planned for our trip. One of the trainees, Polly Clemens of Johnson City, Illinois, became a part of our group, making us a foursome again. A list of rules was drawn up, and all of us dutifully signed, with Rule No 1: Double Dating Only.

The day of our departure I told my sister goodbye, boarded the train, and joined my friends in celebrating this great adventure. It was our first train ride and we were very excited. When things settled down for the night, I pulled out my journal and began a long, long letter to my parents. I told them everything as it had happened, then used the term "we were suddenly shipped out." I learned later that my Mother cried when she read the letter. (Not telling my Mother came back to haunt me when my daughter turned 16.) Of course my parents forgave me, in time.

Our train was met in Washington, D.C., by Ma and Pa Carter who owned the large three-story boarding house where we would be staying. They showed us around town then took us to a large room on the second floor with bay windows. Lucy, Polly, Ruby Jean, and I shared that room with a single bed and chest of drawers for each of us. The one bathroom in the hall was used by all the girls on the floor.

It was an interesting mix of people at the boarding house. There were Government Girls from South Carolina (all 18 years and older). And on the men's floor were five young men from South America and young men from South Carolina. The kitchen and dining room were located in the basement, with long tables and long benches where we had breakfast and the evening meal. The first floor was the parlor where both men and women received their guests. Guests were not allowed above the first floor. Ma Carter checked with us often to see how we were adjusting and was very watchful about her rules.

Our work assignments were as follows: Lucy Quertermous would report to the Pentagon, Ruby Jean Lester at the Navy Building, and Polly and I were assigned the Munitions Building (so named during WWI but had since been converted to record keeping for WWII). My office involved court martials and records of deceased servicemen. One day the name of a Lesterville graduate, William McKibben, came across my desk. He had been killed in action, but I could not tell his parents; military procedure had to be followed.

This was a Civil Service job, and we were paid every two weeks. Our pay had to cover $18 for room & board, streetcar fare, lunches, clothing, and personal. None of us had any training in how to manage money, and we couldn't seem to make it last—except Ruby Jean! When we were down to our last dime, Ruby Jean would go to her Bible where she kept her stash, and draw out $5 for each us until payday.

After we settled into our jobs and could safely maneuver our way around town, Lucy and I enrolled in night school; our first classes were English and Ballet. Later Lucy enrolled in Aeronautics and attended class at the airport. (In 2011, Lucy's grandson was at the Air Force Academy.)

On weekends we tried to see as much of Washington as possible. We visited museums, the White House, war memorials, the Smithsonian, the beautiful parks, sailed on the Potomac, went horseback and bike riding. We spent one day swimming in the ocean at Chesapeake Bay in Mayo, Maryland, and suffered severe sunburn as a result of the salt water.

My brother, Melvin (Buck) Jamison was stationed at the naval base in Norfolk, Virginia, and he and his buddies came often to visit and take us places. Also a cousin, Gene Sencibaugh, had been wounded and was at Walter Reed Hospital. He and some of the other military men from the hospital would come by and visit with us. I was faithful in keeping Dad and Mom informed, and they felt better knowing that my brother was stationed near us. But our first Christmas away from home was a bit difficult for all of us.

By working at the Pentagon, Lucy had an opportunity to meet many people. One day she came home with an invitation to lunch for all four of us for the following Saturday. It seems that a friend of Lucy's boss, Mr. Gallagher, was so fascinated with her tales of these young Missouri gals in Washington, D.C., that his wife very much wanted to meet us. Ma Carter told us that the address was in a very "posh" part of town. We didn't need to be told to dress up for the occasion because that is how we dressed for work each day—heels, the whole bit. We followed directions to the best of our ability and arrived on time. Mrs Gallagher had prepared an excellent luncheon (but I can't remember what it was), then we girls sat on the floor facing the Gallaghers while they peppered us with questions about our home life back in Missouri and Illinois; about our families, what kind of students we were, how we became such good friends, etc. Mr. and Mrs. Gallaher leaned forward, listening to every word and urging us on. I've often wondered what line of work Mr Gallagher was in and if he ever used our story in some way. It would be interesting to know.

Later in the first year, Ruby Jean became ill and couldn't seem to get well. She made the trip back to Missouri, and the next spring, a healthy Ruby Jean returned with the new Lesterville High School graduate, Ruby Moses. Then Lucy returned to Missouri to elope with her childhood sweetheart.

One day while having a soda at the corner drug store, news came over the radio that President Roosevelt had died. He was the only president that I had known in my lifetime and it deeply affected me. I returned to our room with the news, and several of us walked to Lafayette Park, across from the White House, and joined others who had gathered to mourn our President.

Ruby Moses and I were the last of our group to leave Washington, D.C., for Missouri. Ruby had a sister in Jefferson City, and I had lived there for a time as a child. We worked at the Capital City Telephone Company until I met and married Kelly Pelts, a student at University of Missouri in Columbia, Mo.

Ruby Jean, Ruby Moses, Lucy, and I had formed a bond, and in the years that followed, we kept in touch through marriages, births, and deaths. Many years later when we reached that "golden age," I traveled to Washington, D.C., with Lucy and her husband, Bill Chronister. As a special anniversary gift, Bill had the cab driver take us to 1419 Rhode Island, NW, our old Carter home. The neighborhood had changed, but seeing that house again brought back wonderful memories.

After the War years, I did complete my high school requirements and graduated from Business School but I do not recommend to young people that they do it my way. At a time in my life when I was a young widow (29) with three small children, I had to complete my education before getting a job to support them. I moved my family to Cape Girardeau, Missouri, and started work as secretary to the Treasurer at Southeast Missouri State University. Several years later I was promoted to Fringe Benefits Manager, where I worked 30 years until retirement.

When my children were teenagers, I learned that my two sons had a rare disease, Von Hippel-Lindau, that very likely was inherited from their father, who died at age 32. It's called an "orphan" disease because it is so rare that no research is being done on it. Between numerous hospitalizations at Barnes Hospital in St. Louis, and experimental treatments at St. Johns' Hospital in Baltimore, Maryland, my sons managed to complete their education, get married, and each had one child. Jamie died at age 32 and Dana Kelly at age 44. Before Dana Kelly's death, his DNA was taken and compared to other family members. No one in our family has this disease anymore.

In 1993 I enrolled in Dr. Frank Nickell's class on WWII at Southeast Missouri State University in Cape Girardeau. The next spring Dr. Nickell took the class on a 10-day trip to Europe to celebrate the 50th anniversary of D-Day, and we retraced the steps of our GI's. It was a wonderful experience and one of the highlights of my life.

EPILOGUE

Reflecting on our Washington, D.C., trip, we four teenagers were caught up in this wave of patriotic duty sweeping the country, and we wanted to proudly serve our country. That world will never be again.

I believe my early experience on my own strengthened me for the trials ahead and helped me to survive life's battles. This is a part of my life that I treasure and it has been a joy to share with others.

Buck Jamison, his Navy crew, and Mary in 1944. Clock-
wise from far left—Buck, "Red" Cheshire, Jim Magee,
Bill, and Mary.

Mary Pelts lives in Cape Girardeau, Missouri.

130

Poetry

Charlie Sherpa

toward a poetics of lessons-learned

A "lesson" is: knowledge
gained from experience.

A "lesson-learned" is: knowledge
gained from experience

applied to change
individual or group
behavior.

A lesson-learned is "integrated"
when it is shared
with others.

From this ground,
five corollaries grow:

1.
There are no mistakes
except for ignoring results.

2.
Second chances count.
Often, more than firsts.

3.
Risks can be mitigated,
not eliminated.

4.
The safety gods may be appeased
only temporarily. They routinely demand sacrifice.

5.
In war, doing everything right
can still get you killed.

Try not to learn
that last one
the hard way.

Charlie Sherpa

heavy blanket cover fire

heavy blanket cover fire
sounds like a bluegrass band
not a bedspread intended
to weigh my body down:
the restless legs; the crumping
heart; the mind wandering,
wondering, near-panicked among
the crowded dream-gathering; the
diesel-smell haze; the garbage street bags
marking I.E.D.s; and all the what-was-that
distractions; the dread of the next day;
the debris that now weighs my body
down like the drowsy sound
of heavy blanket
cover fire.

Randy Brown embedded with his former Iowa Army National Guard unit as a civilian journalist in Afghanistan, May–June 2011. He authored the poetry collection "Welcome to FOB Haiku: War Poems from Inside the Wire" (Middle West Press, 2015). His work has appeared widely in literary print and online publications. As "Charlie Sherpa," he blogs about military culture at: www.redbullrising.com.

KABOOM

Paliwada is a fifteen minute trip in an armored truck with machine guns mounted. It should have been a quick turn and burn but the lead truck takes a right when it should have been a left onto a street where children without shoes play soccer with garbage balls and throw rocks at gunners in the turrets and are choked by dust kicked up by the vehicles speeding by. FOB Paliwada, named after a West Pointer killed early in the war, with a tank for the gate and guys in sand bagged tents waiting for the mail to come in a truck met by explosions on a dead end road.

Contact left.
Contact Right.

"Where the hell is Paliwada?" It should have been fifteen minutes but gun truck three is on fire and screams from inside are silenced as ammunition cook off and perforate flesh and armor. "Who is closest?" Paliwada. The UAV caught it on camera. Someone in another desert eating take out from a Mexican drive-through watches live as men are pulled from vehicles and their brains blow onto the street. What happens in life when left is right?

Quagmire

Rain drops penetrate the mist.
Fog slips by my face in a silent kiss.

The saturation rings droplets in my hair.
It is a mystery: water in the air.

Water that cleans and heals
Even water that kills in deserts bleeding sweat,

weighed down by body armor
sinking to the depths of the Tigris.

Boots caught in mud and cries muted
by the torrent's afterbirth sluicing

a silted casket of liquid lead
encasing the Humvee left for dead.

What they were looking for was never found.
And here they are delivered home

bound in unadorned bassinets
escorted by uniforms in step.

Each known by flag instead of name and
all is silence but for the rain.

Charity Winters is a 2003 graduate of the United States Air Force Academy and freelance writer. During her six years on active duty as an Air Force Security Forces Officer, she deployed three times to Iraq, conducting security operations. She is currently a graduate student in Austin Peay State University's English program. Her writing has appeared in various publications, including *Proud to Be: Writing by American Warriors* Volume 2 and 4.

Pat O'Regan

The Dead (No. 3)

'Unintentional Self-Destruction,'
The Army calls it.
Shelby—young, bored and alone
In the barracks—did himself in,
While playing with a grenade.
The honor of dying in a war. . .
The heroics of it. . .
So it was for almost a fifth of the names
On the Wall—accidents or friendly fire.

War is all luck.
Had Shelby been given a combat role,
Likely, he'd still be alive,
To see his son's children grow up.
Or the thirteen mortarmen—
Friends from training days—
Safe behind the wire,
Killed when a rocket hit a truckload of ammo.
I was assigned to a combat unit,
Out in the field, being shot at.

War is a mad concoction—young men, flammables,
Explosives, perhaps alcohol and drugs.
Human nature goes to war,
And accidents must happen.
They are casualties, too.
The country sent them, too.
They answered the call, and
Endured the stern embrace of war,
No less than those felled by enemy fire.

No less for the men killed when a bad mortar round
Landed in their ambush position.
No less for the soldier killed when his buddy handed down his rifle,
Muzzle first, for a hand up on a dike.
No less for the guy thrown from a truck
Driven like a hot rod back on the streets,

And smashed beneath the load.
No less for the jeep driver killed when his pet monkey
Pulled the pin on a white phosphorus grenade.
No less for the mortarman who threw a cigarette on charges and
  caught on fire.
And no less for the scared kid who crawled out in front of his ambush
  position
At night to relieve himself—
An officer ordered a 'Recon by fire.'
No less for them a death by war,
Than the unlucky ones caught by slugs or fragments
From the enemy.
All served, all gave all.

War's nature mandates that many must die,
And in a myriad of ways.
But for all, no less the tragedy and
No less the honor.

From a small farming community, Pat O'Regan migrated to the city for college. He earned degrees in history, biology, and a Masters in Zoology. Then he was drafted—combat infantry in Vietnam (199th Brigade). He taught at a small college, finally wrote for business. He has written novels, short stories, essays, and plays. After reconnecting with the men of Vietnam days, he wrote a memoir of his Vietnam tour. Recently, he has been writing poetry.

Abby E. Murray

How to Use Your Arms

I like to think I'd use my arms
to defend my neighbors,
the Hindu prayer nailed to their porch
beneath a rope of Christmas lights.
My mother's mother stops by
to push Russian teacakes into my freezer
and tells me when they were stationed in Turkey
somebody said not to decorate for Christmas
on account of the terrorists,
but every Turk in the building knew
they were Christian and knocked,
hours after dinner, on the apartment door,
asking to see the tree. Of course
she let them in, of course
she offered cookies.
They clasped their hands behind their backs
and stared at the top bough,
the hand-sewn angel,
and said *may we touch this?*
She takes a teacake for herself
before the freezer door shuts.
Now the kindest gestures are weapons,
now darkness imitates a knock on the door.
We study our hands, our soft selves,
and think *machete.* We think *shotgun.*
When I point at the bathroom mirror I can see
the barrel of my index finger is loaded,
bullets hunched in the bone.

Abby E. Murray has an MFA from Pacific University and a Ph.D. in English from
Binghamton University. Finishing Line Press published her second chapbook, *Quick
Draw: Poems from a Soldier's Wife,* in 2012, and her first book, *Hail and Farewell,* is a
finalist in the Four Way Books Intro Prize in Poetry. Abby's husband, an active duty
army officer, is currently stationed at Joint Base Lewis–McChord, and she teaches
creative writing at the University of Washington–Tacoma.

The Church Ruins at Quang Ngai

I see it each morning just south of the river
as I climb to the west to begin my day.
I can look into the church, its roof and west
wall gone, the others damaged. The gothic
windows long have lost their colored glass;
only spidery frames remain. The church
is empty of furniture and debris as if that
has more value than the church. No one I ask
has any idea when the church was destroyed
or why it has never been rebuilt.

It must have been built by French Catholics
before the French were kicked out of Vietnam.
Perhaps the people didn't want to remember
French arrogance or that of the church, so they
never rebuilt that monument to them. Perhaps,
with the horror of many years of war swirling
around their lives, the church became irrelevant.

And so it stands, abandoned. Sampans float
slowly past in the muddy river a hundred yards
from the back wall, farmers shoulder heavy
loads or drive donkey carts on the dirt road
past the front door. The cemetery lies beyond
the destroyed wall, and rice paddies sit green
to the east. That church seems a monument
also to our own foolish arrogance.

Art Elser retired from the Air Force in 1979 after 20 years as a pilot, including a combat tour as a Forward Air Controller in Vietnam, 1967–68. He was a SAC tanker pilot during the Cuban Missile Crisis. He later retired as a technical writer in 2008 and lives in Denver with his wife of 34 years. He has a PhD in English Literature and has taught writing for over 30 years.

Benjamin Busch

Full Bleed

We don't own it, but we have to keep just enough,
a gallon and a half, worry when we see it run.
We'll say, "That's my blood." though we really can't tell
one man's blood from another's.

"That's blood," we say and we'll pause, looking down amazed,
bright on bandages and we'll drop what we're doing,
pay attention, seal the drip that goes all the way to our hearts,
everyone telling us to stay calm.

He was calm, ripped open quiet, the air hard.
Tore holes blood couldn't imagine. On my hand. My boots.
This blood has been in the tips of his fingers,
close enough to touch, warmed by the sun.
Summers in Maine. Summers in the war.
This blood has been in his mind, passed through,
never knew what he thought.

We don't mention the intimacy of blood.
But here in the street when it spills out like this,
drained from wounds it can't seal,
I can feel his blood trying to put a scab on me instead.
Blood tries to save everyone.

This is a full bleed. Given to insects and soil.
And given to me. A new way to see myself,
and I don't know what to do.

The metal's rusting on my arm,
armor forming one color thick, thinner than dust,
cracking in my palm.

Here's where I split apart,
along these life lines,
blood cracking.
These dry palm trees.

Did you know blood could crack?

This is his.

I'll have to wash it off to make sure he's gone.

Benjamin Busch is the author of the memoir, *Dust to Dust* (Ecco). Following his graduation from Vassar College he served as a Marine Corps infantry officer for 16 years, deploying for two combat tours in Iraq where he was wounded in the battle for Ramadi. His poems have appeared in *North American Review, Prairie Schooner, Five Points, The Florida Review, Oberon, Epiphany* and *Michigan Quarterly Review* among others. He lives on a farm in Michigan.

Action Heroes

I learned about heroes watching John Wayne
battle Indians with unflappable demeanor
and same stiff-legged strut he displayed

toward disrespectful cowhands. Forty feet tall,
fear held no sway in his syrupy drawl.
Far from theaters' air-conditioned bliss,

a soldier huddles pale and sweaty outside
a desert bunker, salt-ringed uniform rank as
a dead hog. Around the corner, a sickle waits

to claim another neck. Pure insanity to enter,
but orders are orders. No golden statues
awarded to privates; no stunt doubles to kick

down doors and plunge into the dark;
no screen credits unless they crawl into
a flag-draped box. High cost of every

sand-choked second recognized only in
clenched expressions of soldiers stacked
in line, their turn next to face the blade.

Bill Glose is a former paratrooper and author of three poetry collections, including *Half a Man*, whose poems arise from his experiences as a combat platoon leader in the Gulf War.

Bryan D. Nickerson

Come Back to the World

There's a pill for your arthritic knees
which you got running 3 to 5 miles everyday.
Beating your feet to the sound of cadence.

A pill for your herniated disk
from an clearing op in Afghanistan.
Such a heavy ruck it blew your disk.

Don't forget that pill that is supposed to help you sleep.
The reality is it doesn't help you sleep better
because when you sleep you see old friends.

Some pills for this and that, throw pills at them.
Soon if you're lucky they will go away.
Senseless rate of 22 a day.

No pill to fix a broken picture frame flung against the wall after
a bitter fight about how you don't do enough around the house.
Getting an education and working to pay the bills isn't enough

to end the sobbing and screeching that always flashes you back
to a raid in 2012. Kicking in the door of a compound at noon after
you told the gunner to suppress it as you dropped HEDP in it.

To make your wife want to be with you. After all this time you forgot
how to show her she is your world. You spent so much time worrying
about finances that you don't even know what to get for her birthday.

You can't relate anymore to being a civilian; it doesn't feel right.
You can't understand how people don't move with a purpose to
get a job done or grit their teeth and deal with an inconvenience.

No help to transition out of the military and market your leadership skills
forged in combat. To find a job because apparently all people think
you are good for is killing people and manual labor.

The only place shit made sense was over there.
A simple job, stay alive and bring your men back.

The simple life; god those days seemed too easy now.

Nothing to help you reconnect with loved ones.
Nothing to help you find stability and happiness.
Nothing to help you put back together the life you knew.

Welcome back to The World.

Bryan D. Nickerson was born in Buffalo, New York. He dropped out of college in 2007 to enlist in the Army and served from July 2007 until January 2015. He served as an Airborne Infantryman for one tour in Iraq and three in Afghanistan. Nickerson held most positions from squad leader and below. He has reentered college. He writes out of North Carolina with the love and support of his wife, Laura.

Caleb Nelson

Orange

Sunsets fool with waves in the Gulf.
Dark in divots, cresting orange,
like aluminum foil wrinkling,
reflecting a broiling sunset,
under smoke and clouds glowing bright
with oil stains, ripples the water.

Colorful flashes of water
light a straight path across the Gulf
from this carrier to the bright
horizon, splitting an orange
porthole, or another reset
button, its bottom half wrinkling

into a trail westward, wrinkling
in time, a battle line in water
for the fly in from the left. Set
a course up wind across the Gulf
as they approach in the orange,
just back from bombing Iraq. Bright

night lit deck, I climb up bright
faced, glancing beneath me. Wrinkling
in waves of brown and dim orange
under the catwalk that water
churns and froths at the hull. The Gulf
disappears after the sunset.

Donning cranial and headset
as flight schedule begins in bright
flashes and sparks I cross a gulf
now dark, running with chains wrinkling
on my shoulders, sweating water,
wet eyes, ducking under orange

orbs, avoiding exhaust. Orange
beams bathe the deck, a smile set

around my teeth, with salt water
saliva dry in my cheeks. Bright
flashlights find tie downs. Hook wrinkling
chains up to the jet, in the gulf

of a wheel well, and set bright
orange safety pins, an inkling
my pilot needs water in the Gulf.

Caleb Nelson served in the Navy from 2004 to 2008 as an Aviation Electrician in an F/A-18E squadron. Since graduating with an MA in Creative Writing from UMass–Boston in 2015, he's been writing local news stories for the *Dorchester Reporter* and working on a poetry manuscript. His current blog is 39waystojihad.com.

Chuck Von Nordheim

Self-Portrait #5

Cubicle walls block the outside sunlight in this office
Otherwise I would stare at the melted face across from me
Shadows allow me to discuss CDs lost in shipment
Instead of the lost functionality of arms and legs
Charts exist to derive the value of shipment-cracked guitars
Or to adjust Prong posters military movers ripped
But no tables compare a bomb's blast against a troop's life
Or correct for the unfair dispersal of fates between
Service in Saudi and orders to Edwards Air Force Base

Chuck served in the US Air Force for 22 years as an F-4 radar mechanic and a paralegal from 1987 to 2009. His duty stations included Clark and Kunsan Air Base, a TDY stint at the US Embassy in Baghdad, and stateside assignments at Eglin, Edwards, and Travis Air Force Base. Currently an MFA candidate at CSU San Bernardino, his work has appeared in *Poetry Quarterly*, *Northridge Review*, and *Statements Magazine*.

A. Sean Taylor

Selfie in Iraq

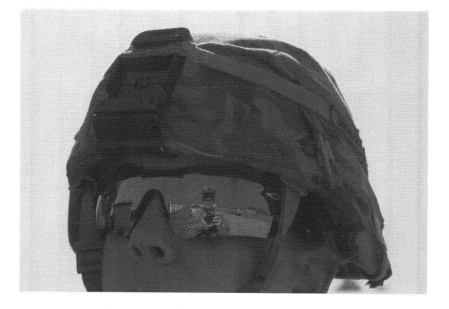

Captain A. Sean Taylor, PAO, 649th RSG, Unites States Army Reserve, Cedar Rapids, Iowa, enlisted with the Iowa Army National Guard on October 24, 2002, at the age of 35. He deployed to Bagram, Afghanistan, with the Iowa Guard from 2010-2011 and just recently returned in 2015 from a deployment to Taji, Iraq, with the 310th ESC Advise and Assist Team supporting the Iraqi Security Forces with their fight against ISIS/ISIL.

Derek Handley

Life Flight

The rotors continue to rotate as prisoner-patients are
carried out the rear of the helo.
Only plastic handcuffs and green camouflage blankets
cover their naked bodies lying on stretchers.

The aircraft seem small but yet they
still keep pouring out
like a string of hornets
fleeing a disturbed nest.

I stand to the side and watch as
the network cameras devour these images
and their handlers ask me for more.
Maybe talk to someone who has been shot.

A blanket flies off one of the patients
excited to be free, it twists and rushes up
through the blender-like rotor blades
chopping it into many little pieces
with one for me to save as a souvenir.

The last person walks slowly out the back,
an American soldier clutching a baby
wrapped tight in a gray blanket that
will never fly away.

These images will continue to play,
as I walk down Fifth Avenue to the Cathedral,
until the large sound of the life flight scurrying overhead
becomes smaller little pieces.

Derek Handley served during Operation Iraqi Freedom as a Navy Public Affairs officer and is currently teaching as an Instructor in the English Department at the United States Naval Academy. He is a PhD candidate in Rhetoric at Carnegie Mellon University, thanks to the Post 9-11 GI Bill. He holds a B.A. in English Arts from Hampton University and an MFA in Creative Writing from the University of Pittsburgh.

Members of Company A

Members of Company A 2/7 Infantry 1st Air Cavalry boarding a helicopter of the 228(Ash) Bn. Closing down firebase Custer headed to Bien Hoa. Photographer Sp 4 James Rifenbark 13 Mar. 71 221Sig Co (Pic) SEPC (South East Asia Pictorial Center).

James Hugo Rifenbark entered the Army in February 1970 and received his M.O.S.,—84 B (still photographer) because of his civilian experience. He served in Vietnam December 1970 to November 1971, working mostly with the 221st Signal Company (Pictoral) 1st Signal Brigade. Writing while in Vietnam was a major help. It kept his head straight and focused on completing his degree once he returned home. He's been married for 38 years and has one daughter.

Hill 471

In Honor of Max Cleland

On the tail end of Operation Ford
and at the genesis
of Pegasus we deployed
by convoy to Ca Lu
which I didn't recall
until I uncovered a document
recounting a chronicle
of my unit's activities
during the '68
Springtime jubilation
of the post-Tet holiday
where would-be poets
from the 1st Marines
and the Flying Horsemen
gleaned inspiration

cowering under the same random crush
of artillery raining out of the looming nearby
green mountainous myth or no myth
"Guns of Navarone" Co Roc

In the years that have followed
a vivid memory of a loose grenade survives
. . . discernibly salient
amid a catalog of trauma

Fred Rosenblum is a poet living with his wife of 42 years in San Diego, California. He served with the 1st Marines in 1968–69, Vietnam, fueling most of what has appeared in numerous publications over the years. His first collection of poetry, *Hollow Tin Jingles*, was released in February of 2014 by the Main Street Rag Publishing Company in Charlotte, NC.

Gordon Kippola

Before Crossing into Iraq

Waiting for something important to do,
I'm bored, counting rounds on my cot,
Faking the confidence Soldiers require
From Chief, and I'm Chief, but I'd be damned
Fine if, for only next year, I were not.

I fight a war that's just kind of a war,
Staring stiff at green, flexible walls.
Too tired for napping, my brain's on a roll
Rehearsing some bullshitty-plausible
Answers to stammer when destiny calls.

Weighed down by my helmet, a flak-vest
Of lead; a black nine-mill strapped to my side.
The niggling restrictions on whom I may shoot;
A bookshelf of triplicate forms to fill out,
Justifying the innocent details of each homicide.

Pushing through hot, dust-filled Kuwaiti sky,
My visions dissolve in a palette of brown.
No scampering sidekick, no Robin-Blue Djinn,
No bantering duets with Princesses,
Climaxed by winning a Sheik's golden crown.

My trivial portion is what I must do;
I salute, it's my gig to obey.
The rhythms compress, the stick breaks

                              The drum. The bugle calls

Death. The Piper hands me his pipe, orders:

                    March these children away from their homes
                    and into the desert to play.

After serving thirty-one years as a musician in the United States Army, including a
year in Iraq as the commander of the First Infantry Division Band, Gordon Kippola
is pursuing an MFA in Creative Writing from the University of Tampa. Following
thirteen military assignment relocations (inside and outside the United States), he
now calls Grapevine, Texas, home.

James Hugo Rifenbark

Two of Us

Thought I was lucky.
Eleven months over there—
no Article 15's,
still stand 6'3", have ten fingers
ten toes. Only my throat tightens
when thunder sounds.
Is it in coming or out going?
Years later my brother says,
his brother never came home.

James Hugo Rifenbark entered the Army in February 1970 and received his M.O.S.,—84 B (still photographer) because of his civilian experience. He served in Vietnam, December 1970 to November 1971, working mostly with the 221st Signal Company (Pictoral) 1st Signal Brigade. Writing while in Vietnam was a major help. It kept his head straight and focused on completing his degree once he returned home. He's been married for 38 years and has one daughter.

Jay Harden

There Is a Time

There was a time,
a time I would have been able
to be in a parade of veterans
and hold my head up
and look direct in the crowd
with a satisfaction that I had done
something with my life,
a time my chest would feel honor,
even believe it.

There was that time.

But time is a changing force,
and that time is a different time
altered by remembrance
and intervening years
past external praise,
past hungriness for approval,
for understanding,
for forgiveness,
and for my forgetting.

Now is a new time, this time.

Now is the time for a different parade,
a better one where I don't march,
where I sit in the stands and watch,
watching one young man go by,
and I understand, I appreciate,
I approve his private marching;
I see fresh in his eyes
and remember every single thing
he has seen, all he did,
and every thrill and break of his heart;
I see his pure striving incompleteness:
the doubt, the hope, the fear,
and the glory;
everything is there.

There is a time.

And in this time, across time,
I send back to him
my silent confirming message:
that nothing is wrong,
that nothing ever was wrong,
that all was given and forgiven
from the beginning,
that life is embraceable still.

Now is the time
we will never be separated again:
now I see his belief in himself
and in something else with his love,
and in a world they intend to create;
now as he turns his head,
he reminds me of who I still am,
just as clear-eyed as ever
and as loyal to him as ever;
now is the time of everything forever all right,
our time now safely home.

After eight years of active duty in the Air Force (including combat in Vietnam), then six years in the Missouri Air National Guard, Mr. Harden completed a career in the Department of Defense, then became a photographer and writer of short stories, poems, and lyrics about love, war, childhood, and personal growth with award-winning work in seven anthologies. He also has taught writing to veterans, but continues to learn from his secret mentors: five grandchildren.

John Rodriguez

Gunfight

snap, crackle, pop,
past your head.
snap, crackle, pop,
thank God I'm not dead.

First rounds come in,
pausing your heart.
Chaos, confusion,
what the hell's happening?
Adrenaline hits,
pounding
to rip
your chest apart.
Thoughts muddled,
unable to convey
a damn thing
over the radio.

Stuttering
rapid fire
can't drown out
the din
regain
fine motor skills
speak.
Your desire,
run away,
curl up in fetal,
pout,
but witnesses
around you
can't be
that weak.

Play stoic
at the post,
just do your best,

hoping like hell
everyone comes safe
through this mess.
The throbbing
slows,
inside your breast
as the bedlam
dies off,
gunshots occur
less.

If your boys
are safe,
you'll find a rush
like none other.
If one's not
you'll cry
write a letter
to his mother.

John Rodriguez was an infantry officer in the U.S. Army from 2006 to 2012. He served in Afghanistan as a Rifle Platoon Leader and Rifle Company Executive Officer in Kunar Province from 2008 to 2009. He currently works and lives in Washington, D.C. His work has been published in *O-Dark Thirty* and *Ash and Bones*.

John Thampi

Out of

the depths of the grave
  are made of these

petrified rock hammered into the rib cage
  soft loam poured into the skull

the stench of decaying trilobites
  filling up nostrils

layers upon layers of colorful minerals
  sprayed into black hills.

the ocean floor long recessed
  there is no where to go.

the glacier has left with relics in its ruin
  where to remain?

these days linger like whispers
  crawling in the ceiling of the brain

like fossilized crystals swirling
  in bottom of a hazel drink

mixing into the white mortar
  mixing into the foundation pillars

corinthian columns every one of them.
  Holding up a blue egg shell roof etched

with the Minotaur snorting
  hamstring muscle clenched

in preparation for an ambush
  I wander touching walls, wet

with dew below the painted stars.
  give me beauty for beauty's sake

the glories of the unseen
  sweeping over the peaks and gullies

slowly stretching like fingers
  across the wilderness.

across the restless street walkers
  across the few resting from

the best of their grand labors
  and bitter travails

what fury!
      can I not still summon

breath and dust from the deepest lair
  force my tongue into shapes

Oh!
      an exhale, a rush of air
  the rattle of bones.

  In the event horizon all quark and bosom dies without a
bugle call

the lines of pallbearers and dignitaries
  the ornamented Cavalry

with sashed princes in stirrups
  mourning for it is right to mourn

sabers drawn
  triggers pulled

for stars are spent cartridges
  of a wonder yet reaching us.

Light passes over the heads of the mourners
  Night has fallen

As the day.
  Were I to remain

I would greet the glories of the unseen
  rising from my bed before the dawn

rising before the cries of the city
  rising again from the depths of the grave.

Oh!
      an exhale, a rush of air
  the rattle of bones.

John Thampi served as Army officer in the Military Police Corps from 2005–2012, deploying twice to Iraq and once, Afghanistan. His first poems debuted in N.Y.U's Veteran Writers Workshop publication *9 Lines*.

Jonathan Tennis

Escape from Guantanamo

I sit inside the new camp
They call it Five.
Before I was in Delta
And before that X-Ray.

Those camps were outdoors,
I could feel the rolling waves of
The ocean crash
A few feet away,
The breeze carrying the salty mist across the rocky beaches.
I could hear the cacophony of birds
Laying claim to whatever the ocean had deposited before them
I could see the sun rising and setting,
Keeping count of the days
Because I had lost it.
I could smell past the scent of whatever we were being fed
To the fast food restaurants just over the hill.

My new camp is different;
I moved in at night
I can scream as loud as I want,
Only I would hear it.

Gone is the ocean
Gone are the birds
Gone is the sun
Gone is the moon
Gone are the Big Macs and root beer floats.

I beat against the walls with my voice
Until I can no longer speak.
In the silence of my steel and concrete home
The blinking of my eyes echoes across my single room.
I've lost track of time,
I've had enough
So I push the button on the wall
Give the guard my name,

My badge number
And he releases me.
He releases me because I'm not a detainee,
I am the detainer.

But GTMO doesn't discriminate
And will never let me go.

Jonathan Tennis served an enlistment in the United States Army from 1998 until 2003, with a deployment to Iraq in support of OIF I. He is a graduate of Eckerd College (BA) and Norwich University (MSIA), resides in Tampa, Florida, where he enjoys writing, reading, year-round sunshine, traveling, and biking with his girlfriend and their elderly dog. He is currently applying to Creative Writing programs to pursue a MFA.

Kanesha Washington

Keep Calm

You serve in all types of weather
and when the tornado of war is spinning out of control
you keep calm with your eye locked on the target
you focus on the security of our nation
as you exhale the wind of courage from your lips
locked and loaded with purpose
you pull the trigger
seconds later, the bullet of battle enters the enemy's flesh with the
message of freedom
they fall upon the sands of time's up
you inhale a breath of mission accomplished
you stand up and move forward for our protection
and the sounds of your footsteps
drum the beat to I'm proud to be an American

Kanesha Washington is a lover of life and people, the wife of an retired solider who protects her everyday, and the mother of a future astronaut. She enjoys all things creative and she tries to live life as simply as possible.

Iraq Before the Storm

Jonathan Tennis

Iraq From Above

Jonathan Tennis served an enlistment in the United States Army from 1998 until 2003, with a deployment to Iraq in support of OIF I. He is a graduate of Eckerd College (BA) and Norwich University (MSIA), resides in Tampa, Florida, where he enjoys writing, reading, year-round sunshine, traveling, and biking with his girlfriend and their elderly dog. He is currently applying to Creative Writing programs to pursue a MFA.

Kent Walker

Gun Baby

I hold my infant son, who was not close
to thirty pounds much like a machine gun
I carried in heat, in sand the dust and wind
I rock them both up and down the halls
here and over there where cries rise up
to kicking legs and cyclical flashes
all in unison to his wailing mouth.
I bounce him limp and aglow like a red
barrel steaming from a roof tops edge.
His head stays down. Don't move. Four shots down
I burp him and ease in several pat, pats—
a function check, he gasps into my arm,
and chokes—I check his breach for a jam
his feed tray mouth is clear of debris.
I shoulder its butt stock, squeeze, and wait
for the whites of his eyes to roll back, back
to sleep—shush hush little man lay down
Know, *brass to the grass with links to the sky.*

Kent Walker currently lives in St. Louis with his wife and son. He received his B.A.
in English at Southeast Missouri State University and his M.F.A. in Fiction at the
University of Missouri–St. Louis. He was a sergeant in the 3rd Infantry Division.
While in the Army, he completed two tours in Iraq, one in 2003 and the other in
2005. His writing is centered about his past military experiences and his family.

Lucia Eclipse Roberts

The soldier isn't the only one who has a sacrifice to gift

Lucia Eclipse Roberts joined the USAF (active duty) on March 5, 2013. She did formal training at Keesler AFB MS and Hurlburt Field, Florida. She is now a 1C5X1 stationed in the Carolinas. She has been writing/doing photography for over 4 years. She is 22 years old, living with her husband, Kevin, and baby daughters, Khaleesi and Harlow.

Leonard Adreon

Sergeant Jimmy

Dedicated to my friend, James Henry Marshall, Korea 1951

On a hill with no name
seven thousand miles from home
Marine Sergeant Jimmy leads his platoon
up a rocky slope
through heavy soaked air
shadowed visibility
his M-1 at the ready

Flashes of light from above
vibration of explosions
staccato sounds of guns
bullets splaying into boulders

Jimmy pulls the pin
hurls the grenade
the blast, bodies fly
one lone soldier staggers out
fires as he falls on soggy earth
Jimmy clutches his chest
face down in the mud
corpsman at his side
hang on, hang on
bleeding stops, signs ok

Sergeant Jimmy looks up
Muffled conversations
the Doctor working intensely
hands moving fast
push, pull, stretch

Eyes clouded, face contorted
he sees his Mom, Dad, Sisters
reaches up to touch smiling faces
A party, bright lights, singing, laughing
the banner, *GOOD LUCK
COME BACK SOON*

Sergeant Jimmy on his way home
seven thousand miles
The plane lands
to family and friends who wait

A wooden box, flag draped
Sergeant Jimmy
twenty-two years old
Marines salute
His journey over

Let every day be
a day to remember
to honor, to give thanks
to Sergeant Jimmy and all those
who gave up a life
a limb, an eye, or more

For all of us

For each of us.

Leonard J. Adreon is from St. Louis, Missouri. He served in the U.S. Navy from 1944 to 1946 and as a corpsman with the First Marine Division in combat in Korea in 1951/1952. He is a graduate of Washington University in St. Louis, married, has three daughters and six grandchildren. He just completed a new book, *Hilltop Doc, A Marine Corpsman Fighting Through the Mud and Blood of the Korean War*.

Lucia Eclipse Roberts

Café in the Desert

Unknown words float by,
And sandy gusts attack my skin
At this cafe in the desert.

The sun burns closer to the ground,
As if the furies of the Sand People
Can strengthen its rays.

Barefoot soldiers at play
For they're only ten years old;
Armored with their forefathers' beliefs.

Foreign customs
Fall on ignorant understanding
And the opposing upbringing of a soldier.

There are questions in the eyes of those
Who are wary and watch me
Try to quench this thirst.

The thirst to not concede to this demon
They think I am or will become,
Thirst to refuel this body that wastes away here,

Thirst to make my country proud and uphold its standards.
Thirst to not lose myself
In this war laden wasteland.

A thirst I'm sure can never be quenched
At this café in the desert.

Lucia Eclipse Roberts joined the USAF (active duty) on March 5, 2013. She did formal training at Keesler AFB MS and Hurlburt Field, FL. She is now a 1C5X1 stationed in the Carolinas. She has been writing/doing photography for over 4 years. She is 22 years old, living with her husband, Kevin, and baby daughters, Khaleesi and Harlow.

Paul Wellman

The Path I've Chosen (Four Months in Fallujah)

I've tightly gripped a human femur bone,
Meat still intact—
Swung in a makeshift game of stickball
With brothers,
Each a mother's son.
I've held a partly decomposed skull,
Ligaments drooping,
Quoting Shakespeare.
If nothing else offered, we've shot dogs,
Defenseless and for sport.
Yet it is my brothers, I,
Who were called patriots and heroes
For the sacrifices made.

Simple convoy rides turned suicide missions,
Armored Humvees tossed like Matchbox toy cars
Rolling over haphazard bombs.
The dead mule on the side of the road?
The empty burlap sack?
The shelves of cocoa powder cans?
Wire!

No calls or letters refresh sanity lost.
Will it ever be regained?

The nature of our work
More than predetermined enemies.
Fighting caramel-colored sand,
Sandblasting tsunamis, high winds,
And cracked, bleeding lips:
My face throbbing.
Houses—broken down and torn—
Made of this sand,
Roads blend in, part of the desert,
Going on Forever;
While the searing sun attempts the work of bullets
With temperatures reaching well above three digits,
Even in the dead of night.

Odors linger,
So foul I have no words to explain them.
Flies grin,
Swarming with delight.

My gear,
Equal to the weight of my body,
Slows me down
When speed is essential to survival;
Until I feel like a duck with clipped wings—
Waiting to be struck down by the clumsiest of hunters:
Imagining my last feeble gasps.

But my greatest fear is knowing
This place that seems a horrific dream
Is reality.
The home I love and fight for,
Seven thousand miles and oceans away,
I am forgetting—
One consoling, comforting detail at a time.

Paul Wellman is a Marine Corps veteran (machine gunner) of the Iraq War and fought in Fallujah. He currently teaches at Brewer High School in Maine as an English teacher. He is married to his best friend since seventh grade who continually urges him to pursue his writing ambitions. The ability to help document the experiences of those who fought in the latest American conflicts means a great deal to him.

Any Soldier

The package was addressed to "Any Soldier." Small, white, one of those standard US postal service boxes, it was dumped in a heap among similar packets known as the weekly donation bundle. It arrived two months after my friend died. His last name was written in red cursive above the sender's address. I selected it purely by chance. I needed toothpaste.

Jim, my stoner friend from college, sent me my first care package, a small manila envelope with no padding and lots of tape. I had just finished my second week of basic training. Inside was a short letter and a mixed cassette tape: "Seasons in the Sun" by Terry Jacks, "Momentary Lapse of Reason" by Pink Floyd. We'd seen the Pink Floyd concert the day before I left for Basic. His note said, "You can do it, dude!"

My second care package came by Overnight Express. By the last week of Ranger School, I was the only one who hadn't received any mail, so I begged Kathryn to send me something. I was hoping we would date, but I almost choked to death eating two packages of Oreos without water.

I hit a flag pole parachuting into Panama during Operation Just Cause and broke my leg. While I recovered at Brookes Army Hospital, the mayor of San Antonio sent me a photo of the Alamo. It came in an official brown envelope and he signed it and wrote "With Thanks" and "We Remember."

The Easter after Desert Shield began my uncle sent a huge box. Everyone in the platoon gathered around, but it wasn't full of chocolate bunnies. Apparently the news back home claimed soldiers protected their rifles from sand using condoms. My uncle's card read, "Protect your rifle!"

An ex-girlfriend sent me a small box while I was at Colombian Commando School. Inside were two Little Debbie Oatmeal Crème Pies, my favorite, which made me smile. There was a nice letter signed, "Be safe. Fondly, Paola."

My first time to Afghanistan, my grandmother sent a plastic gallon bottle of orange juice. My uncle told me she used to send rum in detergent containers during Vietnam, and the soap taste never came out. Orange juice and rum tasted fine to me. I used it to toast my friend EZ when he was killed in a roadside explosion.

Later that same trip, I received a digital camera from a stranger. I took photos of camels carrying cars over the mountain and a sunbathing snow leopard.

My second trip to Afghanistan I set up my support network and received 50 boxes of donations for the Afghan people every week from family members and schools across the United States. I had to pay trucks to deliver the food and clothes and notebooks. One friend also sent me $100 in cash. "Take care, and please pay some teachers."

At the end of that tour, I got divorce papers in a slim white envelope and a letter from my six-year-old son with a crayon drawing of soldiers around a crooked American Flag. "Come home, Dad. I love you."

Now, I have this white box addressed to "Any Soldier" with my dead friend's name above the sender's address. Inside were some chocolate chip granola bars, toothpaste, and a letter. "My brother died last month in Afghanistan. I wanted to show my support for the soldiers he served with. I still miss him. God bless you."

Randall Surles is a Sergeant Major in the US Army and currently has almost 29 years in service. He served with the 3rd Battalion, 75th Ranger Regiment from 1988–1991 during Operation Just Cause and served with the 7th Special Forces Group (Airborne) as a Green Beret for the last 25 years. He is currently stationed in Italy with his family.

Land Mine

It's a bad rap, so let me set the record straight:
I'm not the Antichrist, malevolence incarnate,
but a pet goat. Scapegoat. My chemicals are
no more dangerous than those in your brain,
less grotesque than pesticides and herbicides,
off-the-shelf solvents that, sniffed long enough,
hard enough, have ends no different from mine.

I ambush. What of it? I kill with a sudden clap,
no lingering about and savagery like that visited
on a third-world's insistently malnourished child.
Those who encounter my emphatic declaration
are struck fast, hard in a voice that's final, loud,
and full of limbic pronouncements. In my cry
I announce departures from this life, this war,
this peace, in a hasty, blowing-apart goodbye.

I maim, too, in much the same way as other
human crudities do, but with worse PR.
Don't blame me for pictures of children,
arms, legs gone, half a face erased, what's left
turned to look from photos screaming as photos
sometimes scream at folks. Prizes do not go
to shots of death's less dramatic scenes, say
in unmarked shops where sex or labor slaves
provide backdrop to panoramas of suffering
for which I share no blame. Don't curse me
disingenuously, for though I kill small numbers
haply quickly, I haven't your conscious will.

Rob Jacques

Response to W. S. Merwin's "Unknown Soldier"

facing us under the helmet
a moment before he is killed
he is a child with a question
—*W. S. Merwin*

Face under the helmet has moist lips
and bedroom eyes, doe-like eyes,
so one may surmise hatred found him
before love did. Dicta and dogma's lies
have urged him on to the heroic deed,
his erotic need being war's first victim.

In answer to his question, war took away
his gun, stripped him bare, lubricated him
with sweat and blood, had him prostrate
by other young bodies prepared the same,
the truth becoming painfully obvious as
war's eclectic error-terror turned flame.

Bed or battlefield? Bed of battlefield.
Pillows or stones? Pillows of stones.
Sheets or shrouds? Sheets of shrouds.
War revealed flesh, bones. Bullets spoke
to him in reprimand: Don't entertain a
question whose answer you cannot stand.

Rob Jacques is a technical writer who was raised in northern New England and served in the U.S. Navy. He resides on a rural island in Washington State's Puget Sound, and his poetry appears in literary journals, including *Atlanta Review, Prairie Schooner, Amsterdam Quarterly, Poet Lore, Off the Coast,* and *Assaracus.* A collection of his poems, *Desperate Journey,* will be published by Sibling Rivalry Press in March 2017.

End of Watch

I unlace my boots,
and lie out on the rack.
I can sleep deep tonight,
'cause I know who's got my back.

I never forget,
my battle on the wall.
It's their watch now,
until hand-off or fall.

Always vigilant,
always ready.
One force together,
that's how we hold steady.

May those who went before,
rest in peace tonight.
Your watch is no more,
with the angels, take flight.

Ruth M. Hunt is a Sergeant First Class in the U.S. Army with sixteen years of active-duty service. She and her husband, James, are dual military, have been married over thirteen years, and have two wonderful children. She is the proud daughter of a Vietnam veteran and has two sisters who also honorably served in the Army. She credits her success to the unwavering support and guidance of her family and overall trust in God.

Stacey C. Moss

Aching Head

Silence, arresting darkness broken
Head snaps back, mass crumbles
Emotional turmoil remains unspoken
Thirsty sand beckons life-giving blood.

Life's struggle for one ends
Putrid man's corpse awaits
Sense of morality for another bends
Shooter from the dune disembarks.

Decay immediately moves in
Death has another new home
Disruptive thoughts instantly begin
The regretful hike takes place.

Stench soon quickly invades
Carcass is drawing near
Inner turmoil now cascades
Sand cover brain balls scattered.

Gaping hole replaces back of head
Sand is black with blood
Shooter shortly filled with dread
Bullet accomplished its task.

Enemy's life forever gone
His thoughts have ceased
Shooter's struggle to dawn
Abyss consumes the foe.

Assailant's suffering is no longer
War for him is no more
Shooter's distress grows stronger
The body will return home.

One man's hell ends
His life is extinct

Another man's hell pends
Death's stain is perpetual.

Stacey C. Moss is a United States Air Force PJ veteran who served in the Gulf War. He began writing poetry in April 2016 as part of his PTSD recovery. He had never written poetry prior to attending a Jefferson Barracks VA Creative Writing group. He owes a debt of gratitude to Janie, Rita, and Dr. Rusnack. They have been an integral part of his continuing recovery. Thanks, Janie, for the brainwashing!

Stacey Walker

Grace in War

When you first told me of a man trapped in a tank
on fire burning in war on Christmas, and how you
heard him scream, watched more men on fire release him
                to see, to smell flesh singe—
I cried for you,
for your guilt, and how you felt you too should have been
in there. And now when we fight, I think of him
and I want to light myself and immolate in our bed—
                      the damage
to your soul is done and words cannot sway you
        to my side of the sheets.
You move in action, your pillow a gun.
You told me once it was how you slept on your M16,
and how people steal guns out from under you, but yours
was tethered to your leg. They would have to take you
with them.   But there is no tether here.
    I am in that tank with you now, and we
    are at war, but I am no soldier—
    have no tactical training, and I
    maneuver just on your words—
        I can't be in here
        I need to breathe

I see you there blank and tender.
   You are the pull, the hard pull.
I see the moment your small incandescent fire
   hemorrhages.
Contact with you now is blood and a risk
   of blackened skin.

It is sacrifice.

I instinctively want to test your heat—I want
        to reach to you on your side
        of the bed, but instead

            I see the obliterated tanker
        and the older language that predates me—
        your history of wind, sand, guns. I move in
        too close, too soon. I am not prepared
        for this battle. I am not protected.
My entire flesh exposed, my heart
beats raw. I should have tied
it down, but I do want to burn
here, with you—to know
how to cry for you again.

Stacey Walker is a lecturer at University of Missouri–St. Louis and Jefferson College. She has a B.A. from the University of Missouri–Columbia, an M.A. from Southeast Missouri State University, and an M.F.A. from the University of Missouri–St. Louis. Her writing explores themes of relationships and identity. Her husband was an infantryman sergeant in the Army for six years and served two tours in Iraq, one in 2003 and the other in 2005.

Susan Spindler

Empty Boots

Where are the children?
the ones with feet half-formed, hands with
curved fingers, fragile like the lacy trickle
from a neglected faucet, who spent years in
darkened rooms, the chambers
in their darkened worlds.

Where are the boots of soldiers that
no longer step warily in the Batangen fields dense
with mines, thick with elephant grass six feet high that
razored the leather soles?
Some of them mark the shrines of the fallen.
All are empty now.

Soldiers no longer sleep in hooches though
some nights the leeches crawl the walls
of their dreams. They no longer
bathe in river water poured from orange
containers hanging in the trees.

And what of the land, which did not ask for war?
but swallowed nineteen million gallons of
2,4-D laced with Dioxin and now drinks no more.
The Ca Mau Peninsula left naked.

The feisty bamboo grows back,
swallows the jungle floor.
The mangrove will take one hundred years.
The oleander, its vibrant blooms
hang from its branches like
the weight of sorrow.
Like heads bowed in prayer.

Susan K. Spindler is a nurse who works with veterans at the VA Medical Center in Minneapolis. Most of her writing is inspired by veterans, their stories, and the impact of the Vietnam war on her own life. Her father was a member of both the Naval Air Corps and the Army Air Corps, and was a flight instructor during WWII. She has many memories of his love of flying.

Sheree K. Nielsen

Contemplation

"Contemplation" shows my husband, Russell, deep in thought, as he reflects on the lives of the many U.S. honored soldiers, past and present, and friends lost. The O'Fallon Memorial was dedicated to the public in 2001.

Sheree K. Nielsen is Author/Photographer of the 2015 Da Vinci Eye Award Winner, *Folly Beach Dances*, a "healing" coffee table book about South Carolina, inspired by the rhythm of the sea and her journey with lymphoma. Her award-winning writing, photography, is published in *AAA Southern Traveler*, *AAA Midwest Traveler*, *Missouri Life*, *Modern Magazine (NY)*, *Whispering Angel Books*, *Proud to Be*, anthologies, newspapers, and websites across the nation and Caribbean. She blogs "all things" inspirational at www.shereenielsen.wordpress.com.

Shigé Clark

Molon Labe

The sun has beaten on my back,
This load has bowed my head.
But, even weary in attack,
These forces must be led.

The bog is thick, the mountain high,
My body weak and shaken,
But even under blackest sky,
This foe must still be taken.

The road is long, the work is hard,
And praises here are few.
My broken body may be scarred,
But I must still be true.

And to the bitter end I fight,
For we will never yield.
And I will die, by Soldier's right,
Upon a blood-soaked field.

So even if our foe should find
A way to break us down,
Until the end, we hold the line,
And we will stand our ground.

I cannot keep them from all harm,
But I will not forsake them.
And at the call, "Lay down your arms"
I'll answer, "Come and take them!"

Shigé Clark is a Captain in the U.S. Army, Southern girl to her toes, and lover of all things written word. She has been stationed at Camp Humphreys, Korea, and Fort Campbell, KY, and she deployed to Iraq in the beginning of June 2016. She writes poetry on the side, and wouldn't be able to live without it.

P.O.W.

It was not the enemy but it did rob me.
Captured the thrill of living, by bottle, capped in death.
Two black hawks down and two heads blown up.
I hopscotched to the border of insanity and swayed
the line as a flag.
Repetition made the sandstorm in the hamster
wheel ground hog's day
Military bearing subtly disappearing as things became
personal.
No longer objectively detached, mission forward.
Injuries that would casually creep on age and buckle
the knees still attached yet ripped by shrapnel.
An I.E.D. exploded in the mind and *what am I doing here?*
became the silent creed.
Oil wells did not rain in the lungs that year, only
burning tears from my soul.
Stoic mask only covered the chaos beneath.
My support systems collapsed into the grave, as I
sojourned alone.
Burnt into the night's landscape, to night watch and
helicopter blades screeching in places sleep should be.
Quick reaction force of synapses and neurons attempting
to recover senses.
Quadriceps broken down to build up into muscle failure.
The failure of right foot to not brake before
rolling over an 8 year old boy, 2 shades from my vision.
The prisoner of war on the mind, I became
as shackles followed my wrist.
Spirit broken and binded beyond preparation.
So they fold my flag for me and pronounce
my mind dead.

Takia "Judah" Parham

Where I Left Right Left

It was lying prone in the hot sand,
eyes narrowed to slits aimed at green men
popping out of the ground at 300 yards.
It was between gunpowder and sock blisters.
Between sand-colored boots and Presidential state
of the addresses, of boots on ground war . . . my boots.
In the hangar buried with camel spiders, between
plugged ears and unmanned aerial assault vehicle engines roaring.
5 meters left of sensibilities and color-identified birds.
Dummy rounds blazing smart orange and red burst to perfection
on a playground of targets next to my pillow.
Lost between blackout phone connections to dying family members.
It was resting on the stench of the burn pit and on
the road man-made, traveled 1 mile up and back with the dead.
Battle buddy. Fire man carried in memory.
In the brain splattered on his chest beside his rifle, forever on semi.
It was sewn in the rank of a collapsed lung. Wrapped around
the serrated edge of the kitchen iron my calloused hands gripped in regret.
I left, right, left my mind in Tent City on the Red Cross message.
I left it in the Mediterranean next to the only tear drop in an
ocean cupped in the hands that hold the weight
of the world in palm.

Takia "Judah" Parham is a U.S. Army combat veteran who served in Operation Iraqi Freedom. Diagnosed with PTSD, she is now serving time in the Bedford Hills Correctional Facility of New York. One hundred twenty days after returning to America from war, she entered psychiatric hospitals and is now rehabilitating through the arts until freedom. Her life's been a war zone, but she has triumphed.

Terry Edwards

Trespasser

We were the Trespassers.
Soldiers in a foreign land.
Did the people ask for help?
Some people take advantage, of the monies being spent during war.
We called the people of the land, gooks.
But the meaning of gook is a stranger in a foreign land.
We were the gooks, the trespassers.
There is a lot of money to be made in a war.
Just supplying the armies.
South Vietnamese by day, Viet Cong by night.
Who is the enemy?
We were the enemy.
Trying to force our way of life on them.
All while the warlords make their money.
We were unwanted, over there.
We were unwanted, when we came home.
No one wanted to hear our horrible stories.
It's like, you were a soldier, now, your usefulness has ended.
You are like a torn piece of clothing, with no usefulness.
Everyone has turned their back.
No one wants to be around you.
And that torn cloth will not be repaired. It will be thrown away.
You must make it on your own.
No one will help and a lot will be a hinderance.
No one cares,
You are alone
In a world that is moving on without you.
It's like you were part of a conspiracy, that failed.
And again, you are the trespasser.
The one no one wants.

Being drafted into the Army, in 1967, I served on Hontre Island, just off the coast of Natrang Vietnam. Our camp was home to me, and I was proud of the work I did. When coming home, I found that my country had abandoned me. I have hated all politicians and my country, for betraying me. The Jefferson Barracks writing class has helped me greatly, to deal with my thoughts.

Terry Severhill

[PTSD] On Some Dark Night

When the moon is
not.

When stars light the way,
When memories unbidden come forth.
On some dark night
Awakened at zero-dark-thirty
Somewhere between sanity and dawn. . .
Fugitive shadows grow.

The past comes on some dark night.
Starlight, star bright, first star I see tonight.
I wish I may I wish I might,
Make it home. . .
I'd see a falling star and make the same wish each time;
"Home safe" . . . not wanting anything more or anything less.

Waiting on a hill top—
        Concertina wire—
                Claymores—
                    Waiting—
        On some dark night.

Fog-bamboo-elephant grass-round graves.
Smiling faces of orphans and toothless old women, gold toothed street
  vendors—
Soda? rice, fish, hats, scarves?
Booby traps? On some dark night.
I try not to think of these—as I pad very carefully, quietly—
Feeling naked—not helpless—got my knife, ever constant—
No M-16. No frag, no .38 special pilot's pistol my brother gave me—
He was a door gunner—
Fleeting thoughts as I check out that feeling you get at zero-dark-thirty.

On Some Dark Night
Christ or
Buddha or

Mohamed—
These men don't walk with me on some dark night.
On Some Dark Night I joined an exclusive fraternity of over half million
    Nam combat vets.
Do you understand yet? Our plight?
Instinct—fight or flight!
Try doing little of either, sitting there incoming round after incoming
    round—
Mortars—60 mike mike 81 mike mike—122 mm Katusha rockets
    —snipers—.

I have a nightmare.
This Marine was blown away when his CAP unit was overrun.
His parents kept writing us, asking for his high school ring—
    a remembrance—
We swept the area three times and found .... nothing.
His was a closed, sealed casket funeral.

A sapper put 25 lbs. of dynamite right on top of him.
His ring was blown to hell and gone.
I remember this and find it hard to breathe on some dark night.

On Some Dark Night
There'll be a movie that tells the truth—
About a bunch of scared 18- and 19-year-old kids.
Sylvester Stallone will get his legs blown off with a claymore
And Chuck Norris will step on a ¼ lb. stick of white flake tnt
And the corpsman or medic will run to Chuck Norris 'cause
He knows the difference in the flash, the sound and the fact
That plastic explodes so hot it'll sometimes burn shut the wound.
There'll be a medevac chopper to lift their asses out of there
On some dark night.

On Some Dark Night staring into the coals of a campfire,
Seeing shadows—doors into elsewhen . . . . .
. . . . drifting again to far.
Will my son know what is reflected back from my eyes?
. . . . Can he see into them on some dark night?

Survivors rest.
Wives sleep.

On some dark night
I reach out and touch her. . . .
Ever so lightly. . . . . feeling her warmth,
A special kind of comfort . . . . on some dark night.

On Some Dark Night
When Heroes march—
The dead awake
And shout at midnight madness.
On some dark night
When you look straight ahead and see all around
And it's so quiet at 2:30 a.m. that every soul on earth can hear your
  heart beat—
Each breath taken,
So totally alive—aware—all senses tuned to a perimeter that no longer
  exists.
To cry quietly,
Alone,
On some dark night.

On Some Dark Night
On a wall darker than night
Colder than stone
Etched deeper than any chisel could strike.
Our grief—our pain—our love.
This wall within, not to be revealed except
On Some Dark Night.

If there be any purpose to our war, let it be this:
That we, the best of our generation, bought a decade—
Ten whole years of time—
To find a way out of nuclear madness—
A hollow kind of comfort.

On Some Dark Night,
I wonder how my older brother gets by—
He was an avionics tech and a door gunner.
Me and him and Dad were all Marines in country together—
  separate units.
Had a family reunion in DaNang.
That memory seldom comes on some dark night.

190

On Some Dark Night
When all is remembered and I don't leave anything out—
Then—maybe I'll end it.
On some dark night as tears roll down my cheeks. . . .
Don't mistake my willingness to walk away from a fight as weakness . . .
I survived damnit!!
Don't awaken my wrath on some dark night, when my soul don't care,
And I can't tell the difference 'tween now and then....
You'll lose, On Some Dark Night.

Forgive me.
Too many loud-mouthed rednecks and P.C. liberals
Who "tell it like it is" too damn willing to send someone else's kid
Into the latest hell on some dark night.
Red, White and Blue all turn to shades of gray. . . ..
..............on some dark night.

xxxxxxxxxxxxxxxxxxxxxxxxxxxxxxxxxxxxxxxxxxxxxxxxxxxxxxxxxxxxxx
xxxxxxxxxxxxxxx

Terry began writing, mostly poetry in 1966 but until 2015 hadn't really submitted much of anything, anywhere to be published. Much, but not all reflects his military experience in Vietnam. His father was a Marine combat veteran (WWII, Korea, and combat in Vietnam). Older brother was a Marine door gunner '68–'69 and little brother made it to Desert Storm as a nurse with an Army Reserve medical unit. Let us not forget Mom, who didn't just have her husband and all three sons serve in war, in 1969 she had a husband and her two oldest in country (Nam) all at the same time. Terry dropped in and out of college several times but eventually made a career in the construction industry. He has managed to be published in several journals including one in China (*Red Omnivore*), he was the recipient of the Art Young's Memorial Award for Poetry 2016 (*Garbanzo Literary Journal*), was honored to be included in the 4th edition (2015) of *Proud to Be*. He has or will appear in about six anthologies. Terry resides in Vista, CA, with his best friend and wife of forty years, Mary.

The Letter

I'm sure I wrote that *letter*. I had it on my desk and then in bed before I put it on the nightstand. The words, creating a pain in me, the wound that keeps festering open again, like a curtain flailing in wind. It wants to break glass and breathe. It's been hard getting around at night without any light. I hope for the moon tonight, in order to walk the bean fields and check for vermin. They come every night and feed on the corn. And oh, how I want the girl to forgive me.

The one who let out a cry.

The one who let out a cry when they took her leg. I'm remembering something, I am trying to forget. Or maybe remember. Maybe she wrote the letter from the other side of the world, in that desert. No, it was my handwriting. I'm sure the girl couldn't write her own name. Sometimes I wonder if she's still alive and how her wound is, and if the moon, the same one I see, is over her.

She walks on unsteady sheets of glass.

We are all standing on glass. I must make notes. I keep forgetting things. The power has been out for weeks. The storms came, and now I walk the bean fields at night. Note, don't let out the cry, it will shatter the moon, the one I keep hoping for, the one that will make all this work seem necessary. Note, burn the letter. I'm sure I wrote it. It doesn't make any sense if it was someone else did. Inhabited words. Stuff the wound with paper.

Give freedom to the girl.

I asked the girl to forgive me. It was before they took her leg and the stomach tube. She didn't answer. She became glass and shattered in my dream. I'm going to walk the bean fields tonight and look for her. But I know she's not here. I pick the tiny diamonds out of my hands. I have a wound now. It flaps open and wants to let out the cry. But I shouldn't let it breathe; I should keep stuffing it with paper.

Because I still hope for a moon.

I fear the moon is not coming. How many nights go moonless? I've never kept track before. I fear the girl is lost in the desert, just as I was lost in the fields last night. The lights weren't on in the house to guide me home. I crawled down in that dirt like the vermin I hunt. I should read the letter, out loud, to myself. I thought about this for a while as I sat and stared at glass, tapping my fingers on it, trying to form the words around the cry.

But I kept stopping to close the wound.

Stuff the wound with paper, let it eat words. There is no moon. I am inhabited by a cry. And the girl will never know that I am sorry. I walk on shattered glass, worlds below me. I look down to read it. Read it.

Note, blank page; I never wrote the letter.

Tessa grew up in the Midwest where she served in the Iowa Army National Guard, deploying to Iraq in 2007 and Afghanistan in 2010. She currently works at the U.S. Institute of Peace in Washington, D.C., and holds a Master's Degree in Security Studies from Georgetown University. Tessa writes non-fiction, short stories, and poetry. Her work has appeared in *34th Parallel Magazine*, *0-Dark Thirty*, *Task and Purpose*, and *Foreign Policy's Best Defense* column.

Valerie E. Young

Soldier's Bottle

How do I escape this temptation when addictions such as drinking are
   involved?
I self-medicate, to hide my stress or hurtful situations, as if drinking will
   be resolved

Do I have the power of choice to overcome the constant drugs or the
   drinking?
I just sit back and battle with SELF as it eludes me to constantly thinking

What brought me to this place where I see my addiction as the outcome?
Questions run through my mind; these habits are doing what they must
   and I am being outdone

Outdone by the habits, I wonder who I AM for I have no control over
   this substance abuse
Sometimes I wonder where my strength is and question my sanity or is
   there any use

I know there are programs to help, which there are for me to discover
It's up to me to use AA or S.M.A.R.T therapy for a chance to recover

I was told that a young shark eats everything while older sharks eat what
   they want
Which means be careful about the choices you make or those choices
   will constantly haunt

I must slay this beast, or my life will be complicated or negative vibration
   will continue to overpower me
Grasping control over this situation is crucial; recognizing the effects of
   these habits in order to be free
I must first admit that I have an addiction so I can change and face my
   negative behavior full throttle
This is my testimony of my obsession, it's my story from a Soldier's
   Bottle.

Valerie Elizabeth Young is a veteran of the United States Air Forces. She served approximately ten years, with a deployments in Iraq. She is mother to six-year-old son Sultan and five-year-old daughter VerTRUoz (pronounced Virtuous). She is a Head Start advocate and parent ambassador. Recently she was presented with a national parent of the year award at the Annual Head Start conference in Nashville.

Zachary Lunn
A Contract Flight from Kuwait International Airport

Sounds of the in-flight movie bleed
through the headphones of the LT sitting
next to me, great orchestral
swells moving up and down,
loud then soft. My rifle rests inoperable
under my seat in accordance with
airline protocol. The bolt carrier group of my weapon,
its very heart, sits in my pocket. I rub my thumb
over its steel surface and bring
my hand to my face. Lubricant and cleaner—
mechanical smells of life and death.
Flight attendants walk up
and down the aisles
to unceasing comments of
"wanna join the Mile High Club?" and
"get me a Jack and Coke." Soon we'll
touch down and breathlessly
kiss wives and girlfriends and
whoever else will have us. To feel
something again. But first we turn our
rifles in to the armory and lose our comfortable
reassurance. In the coming
days, months, years,
we find ourselves
haunted by the ghosts of guns slung
over our shoulders, wondering if
it is an accident
that Kuwait International Airport
is abbreviated KWI—
not KIA.

Zachary Lunn is an MFA candidate in fiction at North Carolina State University. He serves as a contributing editor for *Pembroke Magazine*. As a combat medic, Zachary deployed twice to Iraq with the 82nd Airborne Division.

Thomas H. Roussin

National Cemetery

The paved path veered from the avenue
and passed between the stately wrought-iron gates.
The faded asphalt driveway
wound among the shade trees
and well-placed shrubbery,
leading to a lonesome modest structure,
an island amid an ocean of undulating buoys,
Wave after wave in neat rows and columns,
White marble reminders all stand at attention,
paying respect to heroes of today and yesteryear.
An endless sea of anonymous white-caps
begs for guidance through its ordered formation.
The kindly captain of this vast armada
of vigilant watchers
helps navigate to the final position
of the eternally moored.
I am less than a shadow in my stealth,
beyond the radar and sonar of life.
I'm left to wander, roaming at random,
in search of my assigned place
to report for evening muster.

Tom Roussin, a Vietnam Veteran, served as a Navy Musician on the Aircraft Carrier *Intrepid.* He is an alum of Southeast Missouri State University, earning his M.M.E. in 1965. He has performed for many headliners and various musical groups, ranging from country, pop, rock, orchestral, jazz, ballroom, and ethnic. He has written, arranged, and copied music for many venues. He is currently compiling material for his family history.

Fiction

Triathlete Wannabe

When I was 30, I rowed my way across the Atlantic Ocean, Mediterranean Sea, Suez Canal, Red Sea, Indian Ocean and Persian Gulf. The frigate I sailed had converted a corner of a storage hold into a gym of sorts, with just enough room for a rowing machine. As the physical fitness coordinator for our U.S. Navy vessel, I was determined to maintain my level of fitness while deployed in harm's way in the Persian Gulf. I won the Ship's rowing contest by logging the most miles on the machine during our transit to the Persian Gulf to relieve the USS Stark, hit by an Iraqi Exocet missile . . . which leads me to this story.

At 31, my athletic hubris sunk to unfathomable depths when I swam the last leg of a free-style relay at the U.S. Administrative Support Unit (ASU) compound pool in Bahrain. Yeoman First Class (YN1) Brown, our Ship's chronic organizer, desired to gather our finest physical specimens to compete in noble athletic competition against other U.S. military teams visiting the Gulf. YN1 Brown really did cut quite an impressive physical figure, looking like a balding Arnold Schwarzenegger with a pot belly. My physique was more like that of Mowgli from *The Jungle Book*, but he had confidence that I would be a good swimmer since I had recently won the rowing competition. For the third, and final, member of our swim team, YN1 recruited Interior Communications Technician Second Class (I-Cman) Spivey, who looked like Denzel Washington, only more handsome. YN1 didn't know whether or not he could swim, but he looked so good that he just had to have him on the team.

So after 43 days of tanker escort duty and countless hours at battle stations, our Ship finally anchored off-shore from Bahrain to re-supply. YN1 had somehow finagled a shore pass from the skipper for the three of us to go to ASU and represent our Ship against all comers in manly pursuits of aquatic sport.

The Gulf in August defies description—one must live it to believe it. I have a picture of an egg frying on a fantail deck plate in the sun. If one did not like fried eggs, one could always poach it in the steam rising from the stagnant water. The pool at ASU merely condensed the heat into a water-filled boiler. In any case, it did not offer much relief from the sun. It did, however, give incentive to get out of the water as soon as possible.

For our competition, the ASU Marine guards had gathered a team.

Every one of these jarheads had been handpicked for the duty of guarding the nexus of American activity in the Persian Gulf. A Navy Special Forces Team (SEALS) had also taken up station at the poolside in answer to our challenge. The fourth team was composed entirely of women from the USS Sierra that was in the Gulf to repair the USS Stark. They did not particularly look like athletes, but all of us men agreed that they had an unfair advantage due to the distraction they gave us in their bikinis.

In nervous excitement, I-Cman and I huddled with YN1 to get last minute coaching and encouragement. YN1 would swim the first lap of the pool, followed by I-Cman. I would anchor our team to assure victory. I had not yet confided to my team mates that I could not really swim too well. However, I felt confident that conditioning and determination would win the day.

With boisterous bluster, YN1 belly-flopped into the shallow end of the pool at the sound of the starting buzzer. To everyone's amazement he pulled farther ahead of all other contenders with each stroke of his powerful arms. It seemed that his pot belly gave extra buoyancy to float him higher in the water so that he fairly flew. He slapped the hand of I-Cman nearly 25 yards ahead of the nearest competitor to start the second leg of the relay.

I-Cman sure looked good in his art-deco Speedo swim trunks, but he sank like a rock into the water amidst the cannon-ball splash. To our astonishment and dismay, he began running across the shallow end of the pool in some parody of aqua-aerobics. He solved the dilemma of deep water with a dog paddle. Needless to say, I-Cman lost our lead, but he sure looked good as he ran up to me and gave me a high-five to begin the last leg of the race.

With an adrenaline rush, I did my best racing dive, picture perfect in my imagination. With fury I churned the water with great paddle-wheel strokes. I dared not take time to breathe until I reached the turn-around wall. As I came up for air to make my turn, I saw YN1's face inches from the pool side yelling at me, his face seemingly flushed with excitement. "I must be close to regaining the lead," I thought, as I splashed away. Moments later I collided with the shapely form of a Sierra swimmer. "Silly pollywog," thought I, "she must be off course!" Finally I reached the wall and popped up, certain to find our victory celebration underway.

But no, the Seals again had the bragging rights. The Marines had already made dates with the Sierra sirens as they sipped lime coolers at poolside. YN1 was trying to find a corner in which to hide. I-Cman was at the bar, looking good. I was at the side of the pool where I had surfaced. It seems I had pretty much swum in circles in the pool and never reached the turn-around point at the deep end of the pool at all, let alone the finish at the shallow end. YN1 says I had looked like a half drowned pussy cat, flailing around in circles in the water.

It seems that I should keep on dry land when participating in sports.

Brent E. White served 8 years as an MSC Officer and 15 years as Hospital Corpsman. After retirement, he taught for five years at Northwest College of Art. He returned to the Navy in a Civil Service capacity at the start of the second Iraq War. Afterwards, he taught for six years at middle and high schools. Throughout adult life, he has sculpted carousel figures that are found in private collections and on carousels at major tourist attractions around the world.

A Break from the War

We turned off of Iraq's Highway 1 just as the sun was dropping behind the groves of tall dust-coated palm trees to the west. *Home sweet home*, I thought as we pulled through the checkpoint into Camp Taji. I felt relieved, but I knew we would only be here long enough to get our vehicles patched up, grab some ammo, and throw on a clean uniform.

We had been out for days, living in our Strykers and fighting in the streets of Sadr City. The armor on our vehicles was scraped and pockmarked by bullets and shrapnel. The camo nets that hung over our trucks on welded rebar frames were torn and ragged. My slat armor was bent and broken, and the lens on our thermal machine-gun sight had been shattered by a skilled sniper's bullet. Cans for spare water and fuel that rested on the backs of our trucks were filled with bullet holes and no longer useful. Two of our vehicles were limping on flattened tires.

We were a sad-looking bunch, and soldiers and civilian contractors stopped what they were doing and stared as we passed by.

Sergeant First Class Arambula called our platoon leader on the radio, "Maggot 6, this is Maggot 7, over."

"Go ahead, 7," came his reply.

"Hey, Sir, the chow hall stops serving in about 12 mikes; let's get the boys some hot chow."

"Roger that."

Our lead vehicle turned toward Taji's main chow hall. We hadn't gotten a hot meal, a shower, or even a change of clothes in over a week. I looked down from my squad leader's hatch and told the men in my vehicle, "Hey, change of plans. Maggot 7 says we are getting chow before we do anything else."

"Fuck, yeah!" one of my team leaders shouted back.

Outside the chow hall, my gunner Sergeant Taaga lowered the ramp, and we poured out of the vehicle. We removed our body armor, and stretched, feeling light and airy after dropping the weight. Our shirts were sweat-soaked under our heavy vests, and there were white salt rings around our sleeves and just below our belts. Once all of our gear was back inside the Stryker, we grabbed our weapons and walked inside.

As the first soldiers from the platoon moved toward the stack of trays at the start of the serving line, a master sergeant stood up from his seat in front of a large flat-screen TV. With a steaming cup of coffee in his hand and a disapproving look on his face, he approached a few of the men in my platoon. His desert boots were free of mud, and his uniform looked clean and new. He was clean-shaven and had hair clippings in his ears, as he had come straight from the base barber shop before dinner.

"Who is in charge here? You guys can't be coming into the DFAC like this," he protested.

Specialist Haney, a 6'4" black kid from Kansas, wearing a torn combat t-shirt and with a dusty face that made his complexion look a few shades lighter than it actually was, looked up as he grabbed a tray. Ignoring the usual military customs and courtesies, he nodded toward the back of the line and said in a deep bass, "Back there, Sar'nt." He turned toward the food before the angry master sergeant could even respond.

As the men of my platoon started grabbing trays and moving through the line to get a hot meal, the angry master sergeant stomped toward the back of the line, his eyes squinted and brow furrowed, his face and freshly buzzed head growing deeper red with each step. "Who's the platoon sergeant?" he shouted.

Sergeant First Class Arambula stepped out from the back of the line and said, "This is my platoon."

"Hey Sar'nt, you guys can't be coming in here like this. Combat t-shirts aren't allowed to be worn without body armor, and your guys are filthy. They can't be in here where people are trying to eat. You need to get your men out of here."

SFC Arambula glared at him. Struggling to remain calm, he said, "My guys haven't had a hot meal in over a week, and the chow hall closes in a few minutes. You guys want to sit here in a combat zone with your internet, your hot showers, and your laundry service, and then you want to tell us that we can't get a meal because we are too dirty. This is war, Sar'nt. We have been fighting for days, and my men are going to get a hot meal before we go back outside the wire while you sit here all safe and cushy calling home to mama every night and making sure you don't miss Taco Tuesday. Meanwhile, we are out there taking the fight to the enemy, dodging bullets and IEDs and RPGs. My men are going to sit down at a table, and they are going to have a hot meal and soak up some air conditioning."

The master sergeant started to say something and then thought better of it. After stammering for a moment, he finally asked, "Where are you guys coming from?"

SFC AB looked at him and replied, "Sadr City."

The master sergeant looked surprised, and his expression changed. "Sadr City? No shit? Hey man, I didn't know. Get your guys some chow, Sar'nt. What's it like down there?"

All he said was, "It's combat," then he turned to face the front of the line.

The master sergeant took the hint and walked back to his seat. He sounded like he'd met a celebrity when he told the major sitting next to him, "They've been in Sadr City."

I followed my men through the chow line, and we all sat together at a long cafeteria table. It was the first time we had sat down in a *safe* place in over a week. We were free from the weight of our helmets, our weapons, and our body armor. There was no smoke, no explosions, no gunfire. We were dusty and dirty and exhausted, but we had hot food and a place to sit.

When we sat to eat, I noticed how exhausted my soldiers looked. I watched them glancing around the chow hall at the other soldiers, and I knew exactly what they were thinking. *Fucking POGs; sitting here bitching about chow, trying to figure out what movie you'll watch at the rec center tonight. You have no fucking idea.* Our older grunt brothers from Vietnam would have called them REMFs, or Rear Echelon Mother-fuckers. I could see it on their dirty faces.

We were there in a chow hall, on a base where a lot of soldiers spend their entire deployment. It was a brief rest, and we needed it. We looked like hell. Our hands were shaky, and our eyes were circled by dark rings and carried heavy bags. Our backs hurt and our feet ached. We sat quietly, almost in a daze, eating our meals and replaying in our minds close calls from the last several days.

We remained at our table even after the serving line shut down, taking our time eating and just enjoying the down time. Soldiers at nearby tables stared at us and made remarks about how dirty we were, how fucked up our uniforms were, how bad we smelled, and how we shouldn't even be allowed in the chow hall.

The news spread one table at a time, "Those guys just came back from Sadr City," someone whispered.

Then someone quietly informed another group of soldiers sitting nearby, "Holy shit. Those fucking guys were in Sadr City."

"Damn, look at them," another soldier said.

"Fuck that," someone else said.

The stares changed. Now they looked at us in awe, like we were the real deal, warriors just returned from the battlefield.

I nudged one of my team leaders sitting next to me with my elbow, and nodded my head toward the flat screen TV on the wall near the end of our table. A CNN reporter was explaining that Sadr City was not under government control, and he said it was the most dangerous city in Iraq. The men at my table sat, staring at the screen, letting those words sink in, "the most dangerous city in Iraq."

One of my guys at the end of the table said, "Fuck that place."

The screen flashed from the news anchor to footage of a firefight. There on the news, we saw our unit patch on the sleeve of a soldier running past the camera. The cameraman turned the camera, and we saw two of our soldiers taking cover and firing their weapons, exchanging shots with enemy fighters. Some of the guys hooted and hollered. Someone shouted, "Hey Sergeant Fraleigh, look at that shit, you're fucking famous."

Some of the guys clapped and cheered, while others smacked him on the back. "Lookin' good, Frolo," one of the other sergeants said.

Another soldier shouted, "Why do they always get the ugliest motherfuckers on camera?"

Fraleigh laughed and replied, "Fuck you, motherfucker. They just didn't get my good side."

We all laughed. The soldiers at the tables around us just stared, unsure what to think.

After dinner our vehicles were patched up, and we cleaned our weapons and drew more ammunition. We took showers and put on clean uniforms, and some of the guys got an hour or so of sleep before meeting back at our Strykers in the wee hours of the morning. Once everyone was there, we double-checked our equipment, made sure our radios were functioning properly, and prepared to drive back into hell.

The base was still as we drove through the dark streets headed toward the gate. Generators and air conditioners hummed as soldiers slumbered in their beds. By the time they were in line at the omelet bar, we would be back in the streets of Sadr City under enemy fire.

As we rolled through the gate, SGT Fraleigh called over the radio, "Let's go get some, you Motherfuckers."

And we did.

Jarrod L. Taylor served as an infantryman in the U.S. Army from 2000–2009. During that time, he deployed to Uzbekistan and Afghanistan in 2001–2002, Horn of Africa in 2003, Afghanistan in 2004–2005, and Iraq from 2007–2009. He received a BA in History from Eastern Illinois University in 2013, and he currently resides in his hometown of Shelbyville, Kentucky, with his wife and two children.

One Dollar Ride

I was at that party, sitting at the table next to my darling. All the guys were in flight school, young, good-looking, and none of us as smart as we thought or as we became. I didn't smoke or drink then, but that night somehow there was a stub of a cigar in the corner of my mouth. And I was wearing a Lone Ranger mask, except it was bright yellow and glaring, more than my solid red sweater. At least, that's what the photograph shows. Me, I don't remember a thing about that evening with my friends and beautiful wife beside me, radiating that lovely smile that melted me all her life and made every person she ever met a friend.

That remembrance led to remembering this one about my "dollar ride." That's the first flying mission where you have no responsibilities, as a student navigator. You just sit and get familiar with the environment of flight: the view from God's eye, the noise, the vibrations, the smells, and the other sensations like discovered claustrophobia (a career breaker) and airsickness. Really, the dollar ride is necessary for everyone's sake to identify those who don't have the physical or emotional adaptability for an unnatural world in a metal tube trapped miles high with only two ways down, only one of them good.

Well, after war in a little place called Vietnam and other such associated events not suitable for writing here, I, and two others, ended up as instructors back at flight school. Life then became gloriously easy, alternately instructing in a classroom and in the air Monday through Friday with weekends off to gamble at Lake Tahoe, sample seafood in San Francisco, or ogle the nude beach at Half Moon Bay, depending on the whim of our wives who held decision power on our free days.

I had a daring streak in me, something irrepressible, perhaps irresponsible, that I'm sure is the reason I never became a general. When life and the risks of flying got too serious, I didn't.

It was my turn to lead a new class of neophyte navigator wannabes on their dollar ride. I could navigate the training route with my eyes closed. The pilots and I trusted each other completely, so our flight plan was a piece of cake.

I showed up at the aircraft to greet 12 second balloons, all wearing gold rank on their regulation flight suits and blue flight caps with silver trim. Really, those gold bars should have been green to reflect reality.

I greeted them at the ladder in my flight suit, too, except I was wearing a leather flying cap (like Snoopy in the comic strip) with vintage flying goggles down over my eyes and a long white silk scarf around my neck. I did look exceptionally fine violating the uniform regulation, I must say. Those butter bars were aghast at their assigned instructor, their example to follow: me, a captain they had never met. But like all obedient students lacking knowledge, they did not question me about my appearance, utterances, or anything at all. They just looked at each other, puzzled, and climbed aboard with not a word.

This was going to be a memorable flight, more than they knew. I would see to that.

Everyone got strapped in, and we took off to fly straight down the central valley of California and back. The students settled into a false sense of comfort, looking out below and started building that common camaraderie, so vital to the flying brotherhood, without any help from me. I waited, but I had a plan. Secretly zipped into my flight suit was a can of Campbell's Chicken Noodle soup, a P-38 opener, one clear baggie, and a twist tie.

Eventually, I suggested to the herd that it was time to enjoy their boxed flight lunch, since it would be the last time, since if they ever had time to eat it on a training mission again that meant they must be doing something wrong. Of course, I mentioned in passing that a barf bag was always included in the box. And then I emphasized that the ground crew was responsible for all aircraft maintenance except one inviolate tradition: every flyer always cleans up his own spew, no matter their rank or position. The implied lesson, of course, was to not barf: "no barf, no problem, lieutenants, do you read me, over?"

I commenced to walk up and down the aisle of the Convair T-29C, ruminating aloud to no one in particular about getting drunk at the O Club last night and not feeling all that great now. The thing about second lieutenants is that they hang onto every word of a superior officer, anxious after training to learn the unwritten secrets of success in the *real* Air Force. I regaled them slowly with more outlandish, interesting details and a casual care until I had the full attention of my intended audience.

I walked up to the cockpit and stood between the pilots, my back visible to the students, complaining loudly of our previous night together at the bar, pretending to get more and more nauseated. The stick and rudder boys played along.

I palmed my package to the co-pilot who opened the soup and passed it back to me unseen by the brethren behind. Then I started moaning and doubling over, whining about my stupidity last night.

The co-pilot was glancing over his shoulder and murmuring to me the growing entrancement in my students' eyes.

At the magic moment, I let loose a great sound of vomiting, profoundly dramatic, turned left for visibility and brought the baggie to my mouth, bent over, and deftly poured in the can's contents from the right side of my face, unseen by the victims. The co-pilot palmed the evidence. I retched for a suitable time, then tied up the baggie, and screamed in satisfaction, "God, I feel so much better!" Each pilot sympathetically patted me with an Attaboy. I must say, ours was a masterful scene of improvisational theater.

I waited for it . . . then turned with transparent bag in hand and slowly walked down the aisle, the chunks of chicken, noodles, colorful vegetable particles, and broth all sloshing around.

You should have seen their faces: colorless skin, irises completely surrounded by white, jaws opening in slow motion, everyone speechless and focused on me, their superior officer omniscient beyond question, a virtuoso thespian in his power.

About halfway down, I stopped at the palest student and dropped the bag on his desk so he could not avoid staring at the contents. I gotta tell ya, it was another memorable military moment of mine.

I stood there, feeling so much better, and rattled off a series of my best outrageous, off-color fables about Air Force flying foibles. Of course, my audience was obliged to laugh, though their eyes kept drifting back to the sitting bag shimmying with every air bump. You should have been there. I kept feeling more upbeat and funny, spreading the joy, getting a few reluctant nods.

I began to complain of being ravenous because I had forgotten to stop by the flight kitchen and pick up my boxed lunch. Captains, you see, are allowed by rank privilege to forget, but lieutenants obviously are not. I inquired around for a fresh flight lunch, but all were at least partially eaten.

Then, the victory. I picked up my baggie, untied it, and took a deep, deep chug of its contents. I smiled and told the lieutenants how great it tasted a second time, then waited for their suspended disbelief and to see if I would set a new record. On this dollar ride, I hit my all-time high. Six of them hurled in a rippling sequence. You see, I knew from experience that airsickness is contagious in the confined air of a pressurized military cabin at altitude.

Fortunately for them, and a disappointment to me, all six hit their bags. Nobody missed, so no reeking smell, no further infection, no clumsy cleanup.

Before we landed, I announced their initiation experience as a rite of passage but neglected to say it was non-standard, of my own invention. The lieutenants were not pleased, but obliged me with wan smiles and clenched chuckles.

Somewhere today, I am still hated by some taleteller who has certainly embellished the story over the years even better than I have.

That's the necessary funny side of flying for your country, defending it, and sometimes surviving wounds and sharing death. One sobering truth of military life, dancing so close to eternity at expected and unexpected times, is this: humor, however bad, however created, however shared, is sometimes the only remedy. All told, Air Force service for me was a proud yet strange life, impossible to regret or forget.

So, that's the way it happened on that one dollar ride, I swear. You know me by now: you can tell I'd never lie.

After eight years of active duty in the Air Force (including combat in Vietnam), then six years in the Missouri Air National Guard, Mr. Harden completed a career in the Department of Defense, then became a photographer and writer of short stories, poems, and lyrics about love, war, childhood, and personal growth with award-winning work in seven anthologies. He also teaches writing to veterans, but continues to learn from his secret mentors, all five grandchildren.

Shooter

A burst of automatic weapons fire punches the air, heavy staccato. Windows up, A/C on high, I can still hear it as I drive towards tent city. Behind me, no ripping sound as the rounds travel. Something stops them.

I turn the SUV around hard, jabbing at the window button as I strain against the sweaty kevlar neckpiece, trying to see.

Another burst, much clearer. AK-47, bark distinctive, angry, hard.

Who the hell is firing? The only AK is with the Qatari ID checker, and I just drove past him five minutes ago. Amused myself noting his empty transparent plastic magazine.

Light pops, faint. Start to count halfway through—fifteen, I think. Nine millimeter.

Over the base defense radio: "Defender Control, Defender Control, Echo One, we are under attack, I say again, we are under attack. At, um, Echo One Alpha's position."

Echo One Alpha—a single American standing next to the Qatari ID checker, the one with no bullets. Only American without an M-4— Qataris said the long gun was too scary. I let that happen. Agreed over tea.

I just talked to him when I passed. Brown, Senior Airman Brown. Good kid, smart, confident. Didn't tap Brown's armor with my ring to see if he had ceramic plates in. Armor won't stop AK rounds without them. Something stopped these rounds.

Long, straight road sloping down towards the entry control point. Listening over the radio, trying to see for myself, driving fast while time stands still.

"Defender Control to all posts and patrols, be advised, we are at stand-to, I say again, we are at stand-to."

Reach for my mic but knock it off its hook and down between my feet. Yank it up by the cord, struggle to keep my voice low, even, calm.

"Defender Control, Defender Control, Defender One. On-scene at this time, request location of Echo One."

"Defender Control, tell Defender One I'm in the ditch line to his left."

Jump out, run down into the deep, wide ditch with Echo One.

He has his search team and the mobile reserve online, weapons ready. I'm like Brown, no long-gun. Feeling naked, the comfort of the stock against my cheek missing, no optical sight to find targets. Useless.

"What's the situation?"

"Sir, looks like one shooter opened up on One Alpha, I guess about 200 yards forward of the entry control point. We think One Alpha fired back. We got half the mobile reserve moving up to the scene now to secure it. Bad guy is down."

"What about Brown? Was he hit?"

He takes his eyes off his sight for a second and turned his head. "Don't know, Sir. Don't know."

The mobile reserve team splits in two, alternating base of fire and maneuver elements, leapfrogging to form a secure line forward of where the shooting had happened. They call each part of the movement over the radio.

"Mike Romeo One moving forward."

"Confirm one shooter is down. Enemy WIA, copy? WIA."

"Perimeter secure, medics forward now."

Interminable wait. Lie there and sweat. Burning eyes, straining to see.

"Defender Control, Mike Romeo, all secure. Scene is secure at this time."

I move up with Echo One towards the Jersey barrier where Brown stood his post. Moving past it, I see the shooter for the first time.

His head covering and robe stark white, pressed and clean, he seemed to float over the dull, crusty brown of the desert sand.

Nine red polka dots across his torso, perfectly round, growing larger.

He is speaking, asking for something. "Ma. Ma." Water.

He is surreal, cartoon-like, fascinating. I don't feel anything personal about him, not hate, not loathing, not mercy, nothing. All I can really think about is finding Brown. I know the shooter is gonna die. I don't care.

People talking, asking me things, I'm hardly listening. I can't see Brown.

I finally blurt out to no one in particular, "Where's the airman on this post? Where the fuck is Airman Brown?"

"Sir, he's in the tent back at the search area. The medics are working on him."

The flashback I'd been fighting off the last 30 minutes ran over and over in my head as I strode towards the tent, the crunch of the desert crust my only company.

210

A fall day. Cold, raining. Absolutely still at attention, knowing the hardest minutes of my life approached. Deep green grass, soft sheen of the polished aluminum casket, stark colors of the flag draped over it, the whiteness of matched pairs of bearer gloves laid with symmetrical perfection, protecting it, honoring the fallen.

Three flags with thirteen folds, tight and crisp. Three times I marched to the Honor Guard formation, three times back cradling a flag in my arms, precious cargo.

Three times I took a knee, "On behalf of a grateful nation. . . ." By the third time, I didn't know if I could get back to my feet. The stiffness and rigidity of ritual insulates us—until you look someone's mother in the eye. It's close, personal. It can't be otherwise. If I fell, if I fumbled the words, started to cry—failure. Failure to honor the fallen with the dignity they deserve.

I reach the tent. Brown's body armor lies crumpled by the entrance, propped up on a tent post like someone was still wearing it, Velcro nametape and American flag in subdued colors, confirmation they're Brown's. I look at it for signs of bullet holes, but a fold obscures the center, and I'm afraid to touch it, as if it were evidence at a crime scene.

Inside, commotion. There's a cot where the dog handlers sleep when on call with the bomb dogs. Two medics stand with their backs to me, facing the cot. I step forward to see around them, but the right end of the cot is empty where I expect to see boots.

I walk up next to the medic on the right—Brown is sitting on the cot talking with the other medic. My Chief is sitting next to him with his arm over Brown's shoulder. Brown sees me.

"How's it going, Sir?"

"Holy shit, Brown, I'm good. How are you?"

"Sir, I'm pretty much happy as hell to be sittin' here right now."

"Relief" hardly seems adequate. I put that kid in unnecessary danger, and it was pissant luck he wasn't dead. How would I have looked his mother in the eye? I suddenly feel cold when I had been hot, and my knees were weak. I needed to get back outside.

My Chief got up and walked outside with me.

He said, "Boss, the guy drove up to the ID checkpoint and fired at Brown from 25 yards away. Missed with half a magazine, then his AK jammed, so he got out and walked towards Brown while clearing it. Brown and the Qatari dude ducked behind the barricade, and the shooter fired again, another jam. Brown came up over-barricade position and unloaded his M9, all fifteen rounds, nine in the center of mass."

The Chief looked at me in his fatherly way. "Boss, we frickin' dodged a bullet there—like literally."

"Roger that, Chief; Roger that. . . ."

Jeff Bateman is a retired U.S. Air Force Colonel. He teaches U.S. Institutions, Utah History, and American Military History at Utah State University. When he is not teaching or writing, Jeff likes to play the bass, ride his Mustang (the real kind), and work in the garden. Jeff has authored three novels: *No Peace with the Dawn* (with E.B. Wheeler), forthcoming from Cedar Fort Press Fall 2016, *Mogadishu on the Mohave,* and *On the Death Beat,* forthcoming in 2017, Grey Gecko Press.

A. Sean Taylor

Training Iraqis to Fight ISIS/ISIL

Captain A. Sean Taylor, PAO, 649th RSG, Unites States Army Reserve, Cedar Rapids, Iowa, enlisted with the Iowa Army National Guard on October 24, 2002, at the age of 35. He deployed to Bagram, Afghanistan, with the Iowa Guard from 2010-2011 and just recently returned in 2015 from a deployment to Taji, Iraq, with the 310th ESC Advise and Assist Team supporting the Iraqi Security Forces with their fight against ISIS/ISIL.

John LoSasso
Buffalo Soldiers

William Cathay:

Those boys never knew. Only ones who knew were my two cousins, and they never told anyone. Closest I ever came to being found out was on that long march from Fort Arbuckle to Fort Cobb. All them soldiers wondering why I never took my shirt off and why I never just stopped to pee. Leastways, I think that was what some of them was thinking. I used to hold it in for so long I thought I would bust, but it was part of my secret. I had to find a private place. Ninety-six miles is a long way to march without drinking much, but I only took small sips of water and swished it in my mouth before swallowing. That ways my bladder didn't betray me.

I was one of the cooks. In fact, none of us colored soldiers really were given anything to do but labor jobs until they needed us to come save their white asses, like we did that time when Custer was pinned down with his men at Cottonwood Grove. We came riding in from the east and surprised Black Kettle and his warriors. Caught in the middle, they took off, and Custer and his boys were saved. He only lost three men in that battle. Did he thank us? He brought his troops back to Cobb, but when he found out we were camped there, he told Lt. Colonel Bullis to order us to camp outside the fort until his troops were ready to go. Even wanted Lieutenant Flipper, first Black man to graduate from West Point and the Acting Commissary, to pack his bags and sleep outside. Bullis didn't go for that and told Custer, seeing as they had the same rank, so they camped outside the fort rather than mingle with us. They ate my cooking, though. I always added my special sauce to the soup, if you know what I mean. My way of saying, "You're welcome, Lt. Colonel." My bladder never rebelled in the kitchen

They left after a month or so, headed north towards Lakota territory. We were happy to see them go. Especially Fagen. Fagen was born free; he didn't know the master's lash, leastways not until he got into this Army. Fagen spoke to those white boys like they same as he. Most of them took his stuff seeing how he is the best of all these Seminole scouts in our troops. They called him "Boy," like they did the rest of us, but he never responded to disrespect. I watched him cleaning his rifle one morning when two white corporals walked by him and said, "Boy, go fetch us two horses from over by the corral." He just sat there working that rifle of his. They stopped right in front of him and kept saying "Boy this, boy that," and him ignoring them. They called Indians red

214

men, but those two corporals turned redder than any Indian I ever saw. Flipper must have seen the commotion because he came over fast and asked what was going on and Fagen stood up and said, "I am cleaning my rifle, Sir" and snapped a salute. Those white boys looked at Flipper and his stripes and didn't know what to do. They kind of backed up and barely raised their hands to salute Flipper. One of them spit hard into the dust, and the other cursed under his breath talking about "niggers." If Old Bullis had seen this, them crackers would've been in the stockades. Bullis was a Quaker and he didn't take kindly to disrespect, no matter where it came from. That's why them ornery Seminoles would only follow him; ain't no other officer in the Army could handle them Seminoles. And Fagen was the orneriest of them.

But they couldn't do without the rest of us, either. The 38th Infantry was the best damn fighting force in the Territory. Like I said before, we set the stage or came to clean up, but we were always called. Our scouts were mostly Seminole, and they could pick up a trail that was three weeks old, and they didn't need to eat anywhere near as often as other men. Fagen was leaner and more prickly than a Saguaro, as were most of those Seminole Negroes. All us other Negroes stayed in for the thirteen dollars a month, better than anything we could have gotten out there in the "free" world. What was I going to do? Weren't no jobs for free Black men, what you think a Black woman was going to be able to do?

I got sick in the winter at Fort Bayard. My toes turned purple and I could not feel them anymore. We had done a lot of marching and drilling by then. Made me see the doctor when I finally couldn't get up and walk. Once he seen those toes he said I had "neuralgia" and cut them off. He gave me ether and did that surgery. Took me two weeks to recover from that ether and that pain, I had nausea so bad, started throwing up blood. He gave me my discharge, too. Wasn't only my toes he cut off. When he saw what was under my clothes, said my service was up.

I wash clothes now and do some cooking. I served well and still have my Army papers, but they say my being a woman doesn't entitle me to any pension. I was invisible to them then and even more so now. But I keep on. And everybody still loves my soup, even if I don't use my "special sauce" anymore.

John LoSasso is a retired NYC high school teacher. He is the son of a WWII Navy veteran who was present at Normandy and in the Pacific. His brother was an E-4 in the US Army from 1967-1970. He lives in the Bronx, NY, and his writing interests were sparked by his recent enrollment in a workshop called "The Craft of War Writing," led by Jeremy Warneke.

Michael E. Cook

Just Another Old Man

Looking up from his checkout counter he saw a couple of the regular storage unit buyers heading his way. They were both young, tattooed, pierced, and had a hard time keeping their pants pulled up. One was looking off into the distance listening to some kind of music on his earbuds while his buddy, the bigger of the two, plopped a dilapidated cardboard box down on the counter with a loud thunk.

"Hey dude," the big guy slurred. "We got some stuff you may be interested in." He then pulled a few things out of the box and placed them on the counter.

Most of it was just old worthless glassware and a few shelf trinkets that had lost their collectability. The last things they brought out were some military items. The guys knew he had an interest in anything military and would mix it in with other stuff no one would buy, hoping to get a better price for the entire box. At first glance he did not see anything that interested him but began to pick through the items, uncovering a few sets of dog tags and medals. In the bottom of the box were several picture frames that contained a discharge certificate and some World War II news articles.

He pushed it all aside and asked, "Where did you get it?"

Earbud guy had turned off his music and was now leaning on the counter. "Storage unit," he smirked. "Just another old man's stuff."

It was with a lot of restraint he did not knock out earbud guy. Instead he asked, "How much?"

"One hundred," the big guy said.

He turned away saying, "Not interested." But deep down he knew he had to get everything that veteran had left behind. Under no circumstances should these two yahoos keep them, because he knew the medals and papers would wind up in a dumpster somewhere, lost forever. The pair began throwing everything back into the box with no regard to what damage they might do. They stopped and asked him to make an offer.

"Fifty dollars right now, take it or leave it," he said slapping a fifty-dollar bill on the counter. The big guy's hand shot out and he grabbed it. The store was getting busy, so he placed the box behind the counter next to a couple of others.

In the beginning when he opened the store, he was buying estates and storage units as fast as he could, trying to fill all the floor space that

216

wasn't already rented to his vendors. It was easy to get overwhelmed trying to weed through the stockpiles of strangers' lives to find things worthwhile to resell. After ferreting out the saleable items, the remainder was sorted into two piles, and if it was too dirty, too worn, or too broken to be donated to charity, the item was thrown away. Many times he would sit back when he found an antique, like an old toy tin car, and wonder what the child that played with it back in the 1920s was thinking, what his life was like.

He was always coming across military items like bayonets, uniforms, knives, medals, or belts and hats, but they had no personal connection to anyone. Sometimes there were ribbons or military patches, but it was not until he found a cache of flight log books that he began to look more closely at the military items he had accumulated in his various purchases. In one of the many boxes were the log books of a helicopter pilot who served in Vietnam, detailing each flight. There, written in concise detail, was every aspect of each mission. Flight hours, distance, and type of operation. His ears started buzzing and the hairs rose on the back of his neck. Under no circumstances could he sell this pilot's memories online or in his store.

Thinking back, he remembered finding a whole trunk full of military memorabilia in storage unit he bought at auction. That unit was a turning point in his life. It was just a small 3-foot by 4-foot unit full of boxes, dirty clothes, garbage bags, and nasty pots and pans, everything dusty and covered with spider webs. Like everyone else, he was going to pass it up. When no one else bid, he offered $25.00, more as a favor to the owner of the storage unit who would have been stuck with cleaning it out. The guy who rented the unit had been paying on it for over 10 years before he stopped. The storage owners sent him a certified letter to his last known address, but the letter was returned, deceased. That's when it went up for auction.

It was late in the day when he started cleaning the unit out, loading the back of his pickup with junk to put in the dumpster. Most of the clothes were dirty and moldy, not even fit to donate. Many of the boxes contained old cans of soup or beans and boxes of macaroni and cheese that the mice had long since devoured. Some of the boxes held old books and magazines, but they were also ruined by moisture, bugs, and mice. It was not until he got to the back of the unit that he found an old small humpback steamer trunk. He remembered thinking, "Finally! Something I can sell to get back my $25.00!" He put the trunk in the front seat of the truck and headed back to the store. Curiosity got the better of him, and he opened the trunk while at a stop light. Inside he immediately saw several photo albums and a bundle of letters. So sad that all of a man's memories, the stories of his life, were sold at auction. When he got to the store, he filled the dumpster with all the garbage pulled out of the storage unit. He took the trunk into his office and began to search for any kind of forgotten treasure he could make a buck from. He set aside the photo albums and bundles of letters, and found several framed certificates, discharge certificates from the United States Marines. Under those were several small boxes containing medals. Then he found a well-thumbed book, a diary. His first reaction was to throw it away, but something stopped him. He slowly opened the book and saw the date: February 8, 1968, Hue—and the entry—"*God abandoned us today, we took hit after hit, where is the backup?*

Where is our help? Too many are hurt and dead—Why, God?" He turned the pages and again his heart stopped. "*Stanza and Freddy were on each side of me. The Cong just kept coming. We fired and fired but they would not stop. Behind us was the field hospital tent where the medics were working to help the wounded. Under no circumstances were we going to let the Cong get through. When I ran out of ammunition I realized that everything was quiet. We had beat them back. I turned to high-five my buddies! I was the only one left! Why, Dear God!! Why??*"

His hands shaking, he put the diary down. Who was this Marine who apparently died leaving nothing behind but a few medals and a gut-wrenching diary? Right then and there he became determined to learn who this Marine was and find his family. So began the quest—it started with the letters. They were heartbreaking to read. Clearly they were letters he and his wife had sent each other over the years. He learned they had several sons. In the beginning the letters were full of hope and optimism. When he first arrived in Vietnam, there was almost a party atmosphere. As he read the back and forth letters between the husband and wife, he could see the changes in the Marine. After the battle of the Tet Offensive he became more distant and intense. He learned that after a year, the soldier returned home, but quickly volunteered to go back. The Marine did three tours in Vietnam and was wounded twice. By the end of his 3rd tour, his wife wrote him telling him she wanted a divorce. He left the service after his 3rd tour and tried to work it out with his wife, but too many demons were following him. For a long time, he was able to throw himself into the hard, bare-knuckle world of construction, forcing himself to forget what he went through as a Marine. He went through a few periods of being in total control and having a decent relationship with his sons, but those times never lasted. He fell into a pattern of drinking to escape the nightmares. The Marine became mean to everyone around him, eventually to his own kids. After a while they all gave up on him and he lost contact with his family. He was able to get partial disability from the VA for his wounds and exposure to Agent Orange and spent the next few years in an alcoholic fog, working when he could and drinking when he couldn't. In the end he died a lonely old man, forgotten by friends and family.

He read carefully the thoughts of this forgotten Marine and became determined to find his family and let them know he really did love them and explain it was the demons of Vietnam who had taken this man away.

For five months he searched, online and Facebook, looking for the family of the Marine. On a cold January morning he was called to the front of the store to meet someone. He walked up, expecting the visitor to be another picker with some things to sell. Instead he saw two men with serious looks on their faces.

"Sir," one of them said, "we understand that you have been looking for us."

He knew right then these were the sons of the Marine. He nodded, and said, "Come with me." He led them to the back of the store into his office and set the trunk before them.

He looked them in the eye and said, "Guys, here are your father's memories. Please take the time to carefully read and understand what he went through in Vietnam." They nodded, and he left them alone to read and go through their father's meager belongings. Afterward they assured him that they were proud of him. His memory would be passed down to their own children. He would not be another forgotten veteran!

Word was getting around town that he was a buyer of old military items, but not for the reasons everyone thought—that he was making money by selling them. Since that time over five years ago when he found the box of medals and diaries in that storage unit he bought, he worked hard to find the families that belonged to the memories he found tucked away in cardboard boxes and old trunks. Time was one of the things in short supply at his age, he knew that few others could understand how important it was to remember and honor these soldiers.

Over the years he found more and more discarded military items that could be traced to a specific veteran. Sometimes it was easy to locate family members, and most would come to retrieve what he had found. Others would never come or call him back. It was left to him to give those guys some kind of memorial.

He had boxes and boxes of medals, books, certificates, burial flags, diaries, flight logs, and other kinds of personal items. At the back of his store, he dedicated one long room to store and honor the men and women who left behind their memories and valor. It seemed like just a small thing to take care of a few forgotten veterans' items, but the room began to take on a life of its own. Every time he entered the room with more boxes of memories, he felt a presence. Over the years it began to grow. Nothing frightening—in fact it was a reassuring feeling. He felt safer and somehow comforted each time he added to the collection. When he had time he made shelves to hold the boxes. On the back wall he began to stack the triangular wooden boxes that held flags used when veterans were laid to rest. If he found a flag without a case, he would build one. The entire back wall was now full of flags—each one carefully numbered and the name of the veteran engraved on a metal plate attached to it. So many flags over the past couple of years had been found, bought, or left at his store that he began to be overwhelmed. He knew he could take those flags to the local American Legion and they would give them a proper sendoff, but how could you do that to the men and women who earned them?

On each side of the hallway leading to the flags were shelves that contained the medals, diaries, certificates, journals, and flight logs of the veterans. He carefully documented each and every box with all the information he could find about the veteran.

These were the forgotten Heroes. Each of these great men and women had a story to tell. Some were in epic battles; others were working behind the lines to keep our fighting men and women supplied with the best we could provide. As a country the politicians would be the first to stand on a stump and proclaim how proud they and our country were of our veterans. They proclaimed holidays, parades, and great events to honor them. Even the Homeless Vets were getting some kind of temporary recognition from groups and politicians of every kind. But who really honored and remembered those veterans who left this earth with no known family?

Reflecting back, he thought about his own military service. The friends he lost in Vietnam. How his father and uncle would never really talk about WWII and the battles he knew they were in. Those that were in the heat of battle just did not like to talk about it. It was not unusual to find a couple of veterans talking about boot camp and who had the toughest drill sergeant or worst food. Rarely did they talk about the actual battles! The most common response a veteran would give when asked about his service was, "We had a job to do and we did it."

Most of these guys were drafted. They went to war not because they wanted to, but because they had to. Each of the men and women who suffered through WWII, Korea, Vietnam, and the Middle East Conflicts, and countless other battles and police actions around the world, suffer in silence. Their families suffer. All too often the veteran who cannot re-adjust to the civilian world ends up alone, left with nothing but their own feelings and memories of what they went through.

Clearly there seems to be a difference between the veterans of WWII, Korea, Vietnam and the Gulf Conflicts. While the veterans of WWII, and to a lesser degree Korea, suffered from PTSD or Shell Shock or Battle Fatigue, they were better able to handle the mental stress when they returned to civilian life because they had some closure. Their war was ended; they had victory or at least in Korea a draw. Vietnam and all the wars since, run by politicians, leave veterans with a sense of loss. There was no victory or win. In prior wars our nation set out to win. The atomic attack on Japan was not something anyone wanted to do, but it ended the war. Veterans were able to hold their heads high knowing that they had won over the enemy. On a mental basis they seemed to be better equipped to handle the stress since there was an end to the fighting. Vietnam Veterans and Gulf War Veterans have been left dealing with trying to understand why they did the things they were required to do. What was the point of those conflicts? How can you watch your friends and comrades be killed and wounded and kill others for something that never ends? The purpose of war is to win, and win quickly. There is a clear and distinct reason why so many veterans of the post-WWII era suffer from alcohol, drugs, and mental breakdown, and this is why so many die alone.

His small private museum was simply called the Barracks. It was a place for saving and protecting the sacrifices and memories of veterans that were forgotten, those who had no family that could be found to honor and maintain their memory. In the Barracks, they were all together again. Men, Women, Black, White, Asian, Hispanic, Rich, Poor—the true Patriots of America. They may not have agreed with the political winds that put them in danger and caused wars, but they all had a common goal. No matter what happened, they had each other's back, and no force on earth was going to defeat them. They were Soldiers. Unless you have served in the Armed Forces, you will never know the camaraderie and love that the men and women of the Army, Navy, Marines, Air Force, and Coast Guard have for each other and their country. Every day veterans and their families would shop in his store. It was not unusual to see several gathered around the coffee pot drinking his famous "4-day old coffee." There was always good-hearted banter when two or more of the branches of service would gang up on another branch. One thing they all agreed on was they all learned the same thing in the service that helped them while their wives shopped— "Hurry Up and Wait." Often he would see one or two old soldiers standing in his makeshift memorial. They would just stand, lost in their own memories, sometimes reaching to barely touch a flag or a logbook. He wouldn't disturb them, but left them to honor the dead in their own way.

Across the country there are countless memorials that honor veterans in a collective sense, but who honors the individual? He started the "Barracks" to give those undaunted spirits a place to be together, somewhere to store their name and history and the sacrifices they made when no one else cared or survived.

He sat behind his counter, thinking of the coming day when an old woman walked in the store. He knew why she was there. The very frail woman walked up to him and stopped. She slowly and carefully placed on the counter another flag in a wooden triangle box. On top of it she placed some medals and letters. Looking down, he knew that this is what a grateful country had given a mother when she lost her son in Vietnam. She said nothing, looked at him, and tears ran down her cheeks as she turned to leave. He knew there was no one left but him to take care of another hero who gave his life for his country.

A tear ran down his own cheek, a tear from just another old man.

Michael E. Cook, USAF 1972–1979, is the past Chairman of Springfield Veterans Day Parade. He is currently owner of Mikes Unique Collectable & Antique Flea Market, after 30 years working in construction. He is beginning a second career writing juvenile adventure mystery books and freelance magazine articles.

The Army's Debt

Dear Sir,

The purpose of this letter is to explain the injuries sustained by Sergeant First Class Michael Santiago during our deployment to Afghanistan in 2006. I was his supervisor for five years. We deployed to three different continents and conducted over fifty combat missions. I was responsible for his training, his mentoring, and his general health and welfare.

Throughout our time together, SFC Santiago maintained excellent conditioning. He always scored highest on physical fitness tests. Even during our last deployment in 2006, he appeared to be in the best of health. I mention this because that is not how I found SFC Santiago last week during my visit on March 1, 2010.

As Ray typed, he remembered pulling into Mike's driveway last week. He was excited as he walked toward the house, dodging toys in the front lawn. It had been over four years since his last visit. Sitting on the porch, a black haired boy in shorts and a t-shirt stopped playing and watched him approach.

"Andreas?" Ray asked.

The boy nodded shyly, then turned and ran into the house, letting the screen door slam behind him. The last time Ray had seen him he had been two years old and thin as a reed.

Ray rang the doorbell. A pretty brunette came to the door and squinted through the screen.

"Hey, Angie," Ray said, unable to stop the smile that came to his lips.

She yanked open the screen and hugged Ray hard. "Ray, where have you been?" she asked. "It's been too long."

He hugged her back. Angie had put on a few pounds, but she still looked good. She had married Mike during the custody battle for Andreas and hadn't hesitated in adding the sickly baby to their family, making her a super hero in Ray's eyes.

He felt her tears on his neck. "We needed you. Mike needs you," she said softly.

Given that the symptoms associated with his condition began so soon after our return, I can only assume they are connected to events that occurred during our combat tour. Events that I didn't personally witness, but circumstances with which I am familiar.

When the hug broke, he looked into her soft, brown eyes. "What's wrong? Is Mike here?"

She nodded. "He's here." She sniffed back another tear.

She led Ray by the hand down the hallway. Ray had always been impressed by the size of their house. Mike had used all his bonus money for the down payment. He said his family was going to live here forever and he wanted them to be comfortable. "It happened suddenly, about two years ago," Angie explained as they walked. "They said it was a seizure of unknown origin."

Our mission was to capture a Taliban terrorist. The vehicles were stretched out in a small valley for about two miles. I was near the middle and SFC Santiago was at the back riding an ATV. I faintly heard an explosion from the rear before the ambush began. It was quick; the enemy withdrew after only five minutes, and we had received no US casualties that I could determine, though SFC Santiago had not radioed in. It took me nearly thirty minutes to get to the back of the formation where I saw him riding his ATV. He said he was fine, that his radio had been damaged. So we continued with the mission.

Mike was sitting in the living room when they entered. He tried to stand with a cane. Ray rushed around the couch to help. Mike's face drooped on the right side as he smiled with the left. "Ray, man, how are you?" The words slurred like he was waking up from anesthesia. Mike hugged him, leaning with all of his weight, not using the cane at all. They stood there in the living room for almost a full minute before Ray slowly lowered him to the couch.

I take full responsibility for SFC Santiago's injuries. He demonstrated extreme courage by not reporting them. He didn't want to be sent home, didn't want to let the team down, didn't want to leave the team without a medic. I can understand his reasoning, flawed as it was. I probably would have done the same. Also, it was early in the war and we didn't understand Traumatic Head Injuries like we do now. As his leader, though, I should have investigated further since he was closest to the explosion.

"Ray, I'm sorry I didn't t-t-tell you. I knew you. . . ," he paused, squinting his eyes in concentration, then continued. "I knew you would have sent me home. I couldn't do that to you, t-to the t-team."

Tears started to form in Ray's eyes. "I should have known, Mike." He hugged his friend tightly once more. "I should have known," he whispered.

The facts of the incident are these: During the ambush, I lost contact with SFC Santiago for almost forty minutes. During that time, he claims to have been knocked unconscious by the explosion, which blew him off the ATV. He sustained no physical damage because his helmet and body armor protected him, and the rear of the ATV blocked most of the shrapnel, completely destroying his radio. Since he was still dazed, he did not inform me he had lost consciousness. Later on, unknown to me, he self-medicated with pain killers.

"I need you t-t-to write a letter to the medical board, Ray," Mike continued, after Ray helped him sit on the couch. "They are questioning my injuries. They c-c-claim they are not c-c-combat related," he stuttered, "and they are reducing my benefits."

Ray wiped the tears that freely fell down his face.

I have no reason to disbelieve SFC Santiago's story. It is very clear to me that he is physically and mentally a different man. This was a man who could run two miles in less than eleven minutes, and now he can barely walk with a cane. SFC Santiago was a Physician Assistant, he could administer drugs and diagnose diseases, and now he can't talk without stuttering or slurring his words. I have no doubt that his injuries are related to the explosion incident on May 1, 2006. I only wish I had been more observant, a better leader and a better friend, and gotten him the treatment that he needed. I hope that you will see the debt that the military owes SFC Santiago, and allow him to medically retire with full benefits.

Sincerely,
Sergeant Major Ray Mansfield

Randall Surles is a Sergeant Major in the US Army and currently has almost 29 years in service. He served with the 3rd Battalion, 75th Ranger Regiment from 1988–1991 during Operation Just Cause and served with the 7th Special Forces Group (Airborne) as a Green Beret for the last 25 years. He is currently stationed in Italy with his family.

Interviews

Who Conquers Then?*

War is inhumane; it is not our natural disposition. We all know this; veterans especially know it. Yet, strange things continue to happen in war, unexpected revelations about those who serve and survive. What happens, for example, when you meet your mortal enemy across a fire after the battle as Donald L. Vagen did?

The following is a true story told to me by Don, a fellow Vietnam veteran, a memoir he wants to preserve for his son, Sam, and his daughter, Christine. Our interview took place in his home in Affton, Missouri, on January 7, 2016.

Don's story is, for the most part, the same story of all the other young American boys drafted into military service who went to Vietnam. But one important event in his particular story was different, so different he kept it private for a very long time, almost forgotten, until another member of our veteran group rambled on about hating all Vietnamese. In Don's retelling, the story is just as vivid and just as important to him as it was back in 1968.

After basic training at Fort Leonard Wood, Missouri, and advanced individual training at Fort Polk, Louisiana, then a week's leave, Don arrived in South Vietnam that April, just one more green combat infantryman with a rifle in 3rd squad, 3rd Platoon, C Company, 2nd Battalion, 3rd Infantry, attached to the 199th Light Infantry Brigade.

Don was the demolition specialist for the unit, routinely carrying on his back enough destruction to create the mother of all combat headaches: blocks of C-4 plastic explosive, good old TNT, blasting caps, detonation cord, and powder fuses. The C-4 was also very popular with the guys for heating canned C-Rations, if used with care. However, most days he toted a preloaded M67–90 mm Recoilless Rifle, about 50 pounds, accompanied by his shadow assistant gunner hauling the bang.

But that one day was not most days. That day, Don carried his M-16 and a Colt .45 as his platoon headed west up river from the bridge in a South Vietnamese-flagged RAG Boat. Like all grunts, he did not like being boxed in on a boat, particularly a RAG boat. No one in the platoon liked putting their lives directly in the hands of their allies, either. It's important to know the back-story of RAG Boats, and their operation that day, to understand.

River Assault Group Boats are really surplus Higgins Boats from World War II that we later gave to the French in Vietnam, who then left them behind. Higgins Boats are essentially 40-foot barges originally invented (they say) for rumrunners during Prohibition. They found their invaluable purpose in the amphibious landings at Normandy on D-Day, 1944. Don's RAG Boat had a 225–horsepower diesel that maxed out at 12 knots and could run right up a river shoreline, unload GIs, and then depart, all in a few minutes. The steel forward ramp that dropped on the bank protected them heading for shore, but the rest of it felt like a plywood container, irresistible for small arms human target practice when running parallel to the river, as the hundreds of small wooden patches Don saw hinted. The boat gave his platoon a built in motivation to exit with enthusiasm and take their bullet-for-bullet chances with an enemy they could actually see.

The unit's routine mission was to control river traffic and protect the bridge southwest of Saigon, a crucial segment of Highway 4 connecting the capital with its essential breadbasket of rice in the Mekong delta. The French built the original bridge of cast iron, then the enemy destroyed it, then the US replaced it, and now Don's unit protected it — just one more small intention of striving young men that cumulatively make up a war.

A typical search and destroy mission up and down the river was meant to stop enemy activity and resupply of war material, including food. Sometimes the missions started with air cover from gunships, followed by a flotilla of RAG Boats, each one containing at least two South Vietnamese: an officer at the throttle and the ramp operator. They simply delivered grunts ashore, then left the battle.

The mission plan that morning in late summer, 1968, was simple: launch the RAG Boats at first light, then dislodge the enemy from a village on the south side of the river upstream from the bridge. Don's unit suspected that munitions were stored there for an NVA regiment base camp in the area, suggesting a future post-Tet attack on Saigon, one night's march away.

As usual, when solid planning meets harsh reality, that plan goes out the window and survival gets complicated fast, requiring improvisation. Gunfire upstream from the lead boats indicated early enemy contact.

Tide conditions made the slope of the bank dicey for disembarkation. The Vietnamese boat captain for the mission screwed up the landing with insufficient throttle and the falling ramp stopped at near vertical against the bank instead of over it, making it necessary to climb *up* to get out, not a good idea. But Don's boat slipped back into the river anyway, losing all speed and surprise.

Then the same scenario repeated again like a damaged record album, making Don and the others sitting ducks for grenades, cross fire, and opportunistic snipers alert to their intentions.

The platoon leader screamed: "Vagen, we are under attack! Get us on shore and out of here!" Don's instincts took over. He pulled out his pistol and aimed it at the skipper's head, screaming louder, too. However, the skipper seemed insufficiently motivated because the boat slid back into the river a third time. Using wordless initiative as the situation demanded, Don cocked his .45.

This time the boat stuck to shore. Then Don turned his weapon to the ramp operator, who immediately pulled the lever. The ramp still dropped short of level, but they were committed. The platoon swarmed up and out, then swept the village. The firefight ended quickly, but that particular action and its aftermath persisted in Don's memory ever since.

Afterward, the GIs disarmed the village, aided by the indistinguishable enemy soldiers who ditched their weapons in familiar hiding places to fight another day, then blended in with the villagers.

Slowly, the population returned to ordinary activity for the remaining morning. Men, women, children, and the elderly sat around cooking fires and began chattering again while others wandered through their routines. Don's platoon sat, too, shared C-Rations with the population, watched carefully, and waited for their Kit Carson Scout to arrive from headquarters.

Then up walked One Arm Charlie, a local disabled veteran, already well known, smiling and saying "Me VC" to prove again his credibility and lack of malice. Don laughed, but kept his professional prudence, for any villager acting friendly, if given the opportunity, might still kill an American for invading their country and destroying their way of life. Don understood the emotional landscape, momentarily passive. Everyone present knew that GIs could shoot anyone without reprimand if they acted suspiciously.

After four months of combat, Don was seasoned enough to accurately observe behavior and body language on both sides. He had learned that the man you don't understand is the one who kills you before you realize it.

Don didn't know what made him stand out through the low flames and smoke of the campfire. It must have been his eyes. The Vietnamese people don't know western cultural arrogance, and when they are in a position of relative powerlessness, as were the disarmed ones presently sharing C-Rats around the fire, they look down and away, avoiding direct eye contact.

As Don scanned around the entire group, one man stared back from across the fire with an untypical, clear, but unchallenging gaze, as only another soldier would who had fought Americans as an equal. His countenance was so unforgettable, so unlike any previously captured enemy, that Don knew he had never seen such a look before. Each time he scanned the group for danger signs, this man's eyes were waiting for his, seeming to communicate some wordless message. Suspicious and curious, Don motioned him over and called for another GI to bring their Kit Carson Scout translator.

Chieu Hoi (or Open Arms) was a propaganda program of the South Vietnamese government to encourage enemy surrender. The U.S. spread the word using broadcast messages, leaflets and safe conduct passes delivered by artillery and aircraft. During the war, Chieu Hoi was a serious threat to the VC, especially after their severe losses in the early 1968 Tet offensive. During the war, nearly 200,000 combatants quit fighting this way. These voluntary defectors, most of them illiterate peasants, were sent to resettlement camps at Quang Ngai or Da Nang where they received regular food and medical care, practical job training, and some education, especially in the English language. The program aimed to repopulate a future peaceful society, but the best became Kit Carson Scouts and translators. They also helped identify VC among villagers, conduct tactical intelligence interrogations, find booby traps, caves, tunnels, and caches of food and ordinance.

This man had the build of a typical Vietnamese, standing about 5'6". He had some flecks of gray in his black hair and looked about 40, old enough to be Don's father, perhaps a father himself. Like the others, he wore a short sleeve shirt, shorts, and cheap, disposable shower shoes. He looked at Don with an eye-to-eye calm and the complete absence of defeat or victory—or fear. He looked inconspicuous except for his confidence and those eyes.

The man's government identification card gave his name and a home village that was nowhere near this one, and he could not provide a credible reason for being here: clear indications of a combatant. With Don's nod, the scout arrested him and bound his hands to take him to battalion base camp north of Bien Hoa for further questioning.

That could have been the end of the story, but it wasn't. As he was led away, the prisoner asked the scout to call Don over.

That man then began the most improbable conversation with Don along these lines: "I want to thank you for taking me out of the war. You are the only American who ever noticed me. I have always fooled everyone until now, so now I will talk to you."

Don was thinking: even though I've just taken his freedom away, he's thanking me; that just makes no sense. Then Don heard a story he never expected to hear from any enemy.

"I have been at war since I was 13, when I fought alongside my father against the Japanese invaders. Then I fought with the Viet Minh against the French colonials. When they left, I fought with the Viet Cong against the South Vietnamese Army and now their American allies. I have been fighting over 25 years. That is all I know, with nothing to show for it. I see no end to fighting except death. I am tired. I want an ordinary life. I welcome this chance to stop. I am glad you recognized me as a fellow fighter. We have a mutual respect for each other. I'm willing to go to prison. Maybe you saved my life."

Because the prisoner arranged his confessional conversation away from the other villagers, he knew his fellow VC would see him as one more captured prisoner and not seek reprisal.

Don admired his long and clever survival, and wished him luck as they parted. That was the last he saw of this memorable man.

In just a few minutes, the war changed them both forever. This man, his prisoner, surrendered and gained a new chance at life, while Don simply paid attention, gaining a renewed humanity and a better perception of the enemy never imagined on the battlefield, the last place he expected either.

All the years since, Don thought about him, this man whose name he does not remember, wondering if he ever had a future or a family, wishing he could somehow meet him again to learn how his life turned out, and to tell him the same.

That's Don's story. He still wonders why it happened. He wonders about the different outcome if he had not called for the scout. Don helped his enemy stop fighting without creating a new casualty, so they both won a victory. But how can both sides win at war? How does that work? Who conquers then?

Don prefers to believe that this man found the life he was seeking, just as Don did after discharge in Oakland, California, in June of 1969.

As for me, the privileged recorder of Don's story, his nearby buddy in Vietnam the same year, possibly as close as five miles overhead in my B-52 out of sight and unheard until my bombs fell to help grunts on the ground . . . well, I found my own value in secondhand learning. Sparks of humanity still dwell within the inherent brutality of war, waiting to be discovered. We pass these sparks along, as Don has done, by telling stories like this to a wanting world.

Donald L. Vagen died on July 4, 2016, from an extended battle with pancreatic cancer. He left as he lived, a loyal friend to others and an honored one to me. Welcome home, my faithful warrior brother.

After eight years of active duty in the Air Force (including combat in Vietnam), then six years in the Missouri Air National Guard, Mr. Harden completed a career in the Department of Defense, then became a photographer and writer of short stories, poems, and lyrics about love, war, childhood, and personal growth with award-winning work in seven anthologies. He also teaches writing to veterans, but continues to learn from his secret mentors, all five grandchildren.

Travis Klempan

NISMO Pearl Harbor

Travis Klempan served in the Navy as a Hospital Corpsman and Surface Warfare Officer. A graduate of the United States Naval Academy, he is currently pursuing an MFA in Creative Writing and Poetics from the Jack Kerouac School of Disembodied Poetics at Naropa University in Boulder, Colorado.

Bob Johnson

Black Hawk Bob: Interview of Command Sergeant Major Gallagher at his home in Savannah, Georgia, in March 2004

Bob Gallagher should not have survived infancy. Sickly with heart problems, his future was bleak and only to turn worse in a Dickensian way when his mother died while he was still a child. Born on July 27, 1962, in Bayonne, New Jersey, Gallagher grew up 60 miles to the south in Toms River, facing a life of limitations and disadvantage. But Bob Gallagher would not have it and, like Theodore Roosevelt, rose beyond his inheritance of ill health and weakness, and built himself into a man. And although he did not escape further tragedy later in life, he did survive his childhood and became one of America's Army's most famous soldiers, known as Black Hawk Bob.

The Black Hawk nickname came from his participation in the Black Hawk Down incident made famous in the book of the same name by Mark Bowden and later the academy award-winning movie by Ridley Scott. Mogadishu was not his first combat and would not be his last. But his fateful birth did catch up with him and he died on October 13, 2014, at the age of 52, of heart problems after a life no one expected would have lasted that long after such a rough start. If anything, Bob Gallagher proved that you could overcome any hardship, even those made by God.

He didn't make it easy on himself either. An indifferent student, he traded his studies for motocross, a sport he loved, after he willed himself to good health. He soon dropped out of high school to join the Army. As a high school dropout, he took what he could get, and that was straight leg infantry at Fort Drum, New York. His dream of elite units, of jumping out of airplanes, was squashed because those assignments were for those with high school graduate or college on their transcripts and records free of blemish. Bob was a dropout from Jersey, a dirt biker with an attitude and not the guy you put on recruiting posters, not when he enlisted as a scrawny youth with little promise. Years later, however, he *was* the guy you put on recruiting posters and even magazine covers, and he looked, and behaved, every bit a soldier.

So Bob grew up in the old school, knock-about Army. He was an early member of the newly reactivated 10th Mountain Division. Knowing his route to the elite paratrooper ranks was through proving himself as an infantryman, Bob worked hard at his skills, and asked and asked again and eventually secured a berth at airborne and later ranger training. And then admittance to the famed 75th Ranger Regiment in which his baptism of fire was in Operation Just Cause in Panama in December 1989. But the battle for Mogadishu stands prominent in the life of Bob Gallagher and overshadows Panama and even Iraq, where Bob earned even more fame plus a Silver Star and an iconic photograph published in the *Wall Street Journal*.

It took Gallagher five years to get a slot in the Ranger Regiment. His first job was as a squad leader in Alpha Company of the 3rd Ranger Battalion at Fort Benning, Georgia. His platoon's specialty included combat operations using motorcycles, a perfect fit with his favorite sport from high school.

And although he loved motorcycles and went on many long rides with his wife, it was on one such trip with his wife Joelle that she was killed right in front of him. He suffered, convalesced, and took to drinking, settling into a dark depression.

However, on December 17, 1989, Gallagher had just returned from a training exercise in Florida when he was alerted for Operation Just Cause in Panama. He decided right then and there that he had to get over the death of his wife, and soldier on. Three days later, just after midnight, he jumped out of a C-130 at 500 feet into the sweet jungle air. As he left the aircraft, his first thoughts were,

"Whoa, the ground's pretty close . . . I began to see tracers, .50 cal, small arms that were going up into the aircraft, and to look down, you could see small gun fights here and there . . . there were cars, it (the drop zone) was divided by a highway (the Pan American Highway) . . . people were hitting the ground . . . and stopping the vehicles . . . the vehicles were as much a threat to us as the enemy was . . . there were enemy personnel trying to exfil[trate.]"

Gallagher landed next to the highway, right between the enemy and his fellow rangers. He quickly got out of his parachute harness and crawled back towards the rangers. His mission was to secure the highway and thus the drop zone. Earlier, Gallagher had split his squad into two groups, five that jumped with him and the rest that air-landed later with the vehicles. His airborne element stayed at the drop zone until mid-day and later linked up with the air-land element.

The next day, the company went to Howard Air Force base where they started what became six raids, about one every three days. Each raid was preceded by psychological operations that convinced four of the six targets to surrender before the rangers arrived. On Christmas day, Gallagher's unit assaulted the home of the number two man in Manuel Noriega's military, capturing him. On a later mission, they assaulted a prison on an island, releasing about 700 prisoners, many of whom who had HIV/AIDs. He redeployed to Fort Benning in mid-January 1990.

With his promotion to Sergeant First Class, Gallagher was reassigned to Bravo Company as platoon sergeant of the 3rd platoon. In his first year with Bravo Company, he deployed to Korea, 29 Palms, Panama, Thailand, and England. In August of 1991, Iraq invaded Kuwait and the company was assigned a contingency mission that they practiced for three months. However, it was cancelled and the unit never deployed. It was a sad time for the rangers, left out of the only war in town.

In August of 1993, Bravo Company deployed to Somalia as part of Task Force Ranger. Gallagher had a new platoon leader, Larry Moore, who was prior service enlisted. Between him and Gallagher, they had ten years of ranger experience. The Bravo Company commander, Mike Steele, was new to the rangers. Upon arrival in Mogadishu, Steele reorganized the platoon specialties so that Gallagher's platoon shifted from primarily airborne and air assault operations to a platoon that specialized in vehicles and motorcycles. Although Gallagher was an expert in motorcycles, the platoon itself required additional training with, as Gallagher put it, "a sharp learning curve."

While both disappointed and challenged by the new assignment, Gallagher and his platoon felt fortunate because they went into the city almost every day and "got a lot of trigger time and into a lot of gun fights." The other platoons had to wait for actual missions while Gallagher's platoon provided security for every convoy leaving their compound. From August until October 3, the Task Force had been assigned only seven actual "missions" in which the entire company went out, Gallagher's vehicles on the ground and the others by helicopter.

Gallagher's platoon was broken down into three escort teams of two Humvees each, often with all three teams out at one time in three different directions. They received their first casualty when a convoy got into a near ambush with twelve Somalis. They broke through the ambush but a ranger, Specialist Anderson, was wounded by shrapnel to his knee from an RPG.

October 3, 1993, started as a sleepy Sunday in Mogadishu. The rangers generally took it easy on Sundays, playing volleyball or swimming in the ocean.

At 8:30 that Sunday morning, a Humvee from another unit went into the city unescorted and came under attack. The headquarters at

Task Force Ranger, including Major General Bill Garrison, heard the radio traffic and offered assistance from the rangers. It was turned down, and eventually all four on board were killed. It was foreboding a terrible day in Mogadishu.

Later that morning, Gallagher's platoon leader Larry Moore had volunteered to escort a truck into the city to get water for the base. Just after he left, the rangers were alerted for a raid that was to start in 45 minutes. With no chance that Moore would return in time for the raid, Gallagher took over as platoon leader of 3rd platoon, Bravo Company of 3/75th Rangers.

The mission alert came in at 2:15 p.m. The rangers had conducted seven previous raids with no problems, and this one was considered no different than the others. With the short notice of the missions, Lieutenant Moore had missed one of the earlier raids as well. Then as now, Gallagher would fill in as platoon leader. Gallagher worked with Lieutenant Colonel (LTC) Danny McKnight, the ranger battalion commander, to prepare the platoon for the convoy. They were, however, two vehicles short because they were with Moore, and he would not return before the mission kicked off at 3:00 p.m.

The mission was broken down into three elements: assaulters, security, and the ground element. Gallagher's platoon, minus the platoon leader and the two vehicles with him, made up the ground element. It included six (of the eight assigned) armed Humvees and three 5-ton trucks plus McKnight's own Humvee and two more Humvees from the Army Special Forces–Delta team for a total of 12 vehicles. The assaulters, Special Forces–Delta soldiers, were to grab members of the warlord Mohamed Farrah Aidid's leadership during a meeting in a hotel while the security element, parts of the other two ranger platoons in the company, secured the four corners around the building. The assaulters and security elements came in by helicopter and fast roped onto the ground or roof. The ground force's mission, with Gallagher in charge, was to pick up the assaulters, the security element, and what became 27 captured Somalis, and bring them back to the airport base. The whole mission was to last about 30 minutes.

The convoy was configured with two armed Humvees in front, then LTC McKnight, then Gallagher, followed by the three 5-tons with another Humvee between them and finally the last three Humvees. When they arrived at the pick-up point, the security element and assaulters had been there for about three minutes. PFC Todd Blackburn, one of the security element and newly assigned to the unit on his first mission, had fallen off the fast rope and was seriously injured. LTC

McKnight decided to send Blackburn back to base with two of the lead Humvees plus another trailing Humvee for protection. In the immediate context of rapidly unfolding events, it was policy to not send Humvees alone in the city. Plus four American soldiers had been killed that morning violating that rule.

Gallagher, however, was busy loading up the Somali EPWs (enemy prisoners of war) on the 5-tons and was unaware of Blackburn's injury and, more importantly, the loss of three of his vehicles, making up, as Gallagher said, "one-third of my combat power." Flex cuffing the Somalis created an unexpected problem that slowed down the mission as well. With their hands tied behind their back, the Somalis couldn't lift themselves into the back of the 5-tons nor could the EPWs inside help those getting in. Each prisoner had to be shoved into the trucks by an increasingly smaller number of rangers. By this time, the convoy had come under attack and started taking casualties.

In the middle of this, Gallagher's driver told him that one of his squad leaders, Sergeant Jeff Struecker was on the radio. Gallagher said,

"I went over and Struecker said 'I have one friendly KIA' and I remember, I was on the side of the vehicle and I said, 'What ... are you taking about?'"

Thinking that Struecker was still with the lead vehicle in front of the building, Gallagher said,

"Who was it? Struecker came back and said it was (Sergeant Dominick) Pilla. Gallagher then asked Struecker,

"Where are you at?"

"It's like I don't know where my own forces were." Gallagher said ,as he finally realized that Struecker had been sent back with Blackburn with two other vehicles.

Coming with two less vehicles to begin with and now losing three more, Gallagher saw that the convoy was getting into deep trouble. Then McKnight told him,

"An aircraft went down, change of mission, we're going to go to the crash site."

With this, Gallagher started to pick up the rangers from two of the four chalks (sections) that were occupying the blocking positions around the objective. By this time, an RPG had hit one of the three 5-ton trucks. Gallagher decided to blow the truck up rather than leave it. One of the remaining 5-ton trucks was full of EPWs and the other full of rangers.

Realizing that he was short-handed but still needed guards for the EPWs, Gallagher decided to put his "mobility casualties, there were three or four of them, guys who were shot in the legs, put them on the truck with the EPWs, that would free up the assault personnel to get out and fight . . . this way the wounded guys could . . . guard the prisoners- they just lost their mobility."

PFC Richard Kowalewski, one of Gallagher's men, was fatally wounded after being hit by an RPG. The rocket, however, didn't explode and was lodged in his body. Gallagher put Kowalewski in the 5-ton truck with the EPWs and placed sandbags around his body in case the RPG went off.

Meanwhile, McKnight told Gallagher to move out for the crash site while McKnight immediately left in his vehicle. However, Gallagher's guys were still displaced and, as he described it, "Spread out about a quarter mile apart, having their own little gunfights going, so you have to give them time to break contact and get uploaded."

It took about five minutes to get everyone back into the vehicles and ready to go. However, when McKnight turned the corner to leave, his vehicle was immediately stitched by machine-gun fire, and he quickly came back to the convoy, which was now ready to move out.

Gallagher described the scene, attempting to get to the crash site:

> "Everything looks fine in the movies but, in reality, when you have a .50 caliber machine gun shooting three feet above your head and you've been hit with RPGs, loud explosions, what's the first thing you lose? Your hearing. So, you're on the radio and you have all this going on and you don't hear everything. LTC McKnight is taking directions from aviation assets on how to maneuver to [the crash site] and simultaneously, Struecker is back at the compound, Lieutenant Moore is back at the compound so there's five more gun jeeps [Humvees]. They deploy them to come link up with us and they're giving him [Moore] directions via the radio also, so you hear on the radio amidst everything else, 'Turn Right,' so LTC McKnight turns right, Lieutenant Moore turns right. So we kinda lost our way...."

Gallagher continued,

> "It came to a point in time when I went up to LTC McKnight, by this time I was wounded three times, a gunshot wound to my hand, elbow, and in my back got some shrapnel, but more significantly, I still had my mobility although

I couldn't hold a gun; I could still lead and command and control. But more importantly, my men, I had a significant amount of wounded, at the end of the day; 32 were wounded and seven were killed out of my [52 man] element. Along with the injuries was our ammunition count significantly low, we started out, we had our vehicles kitted out with each vehicle had 1,600 .50 cal rounds, 400 Mark-19 [automatic grenade launcher] rounds, cases of small arms, linked, ball and each shooter had at least 10–12 magazines on them [but now we] were down to at least, each vehicle had less than 100 rounds .50 cal, maybe 20 Mark-19 rounds and we were nowhere in sight of the objective, of the aircraft plus significant amount of wounds and our vehicles were almost to the point of where they were dying, like mine, every tire was flat, I had been hit by three RPGs, one impacted on the door, one was shot so close it went into the chassis, didn't blow up, continued through and exited on the other side and the third one impacted on one of my men's ["Griz" Martin] body armor inside the vehicle, killing him, blowing a bunch of people out..."

By now Gallagher had 14 soldiers on his Humvee, half of them wounded or dead. He continued,

"We reached a point where we would have created more problems for the task force and at that time, these guys [the other two chalks on foot] had gotten to the aircraft on foot. The convoy had to turn around at one time and continued to take casualties. We were attrited very badly.... A vehicle that is unable to move, that is inoperable is no different than a helicopter that has crashed, you still have a crew [and passengers to rescue]."

Reporting that the convoy was not going to make it, it was ordered to return back to base. On the way back, a crowd of about 200 Somalis tried to stop the convoy at a traffic circle. Gallagher saw an ambush being set up and ordered his machine gunners to open up on the crowd, which "parted like the Red Sea." As they approached the airfield, soldiers from the 10th Mountain Division, which had been deployed as a quick reaction force, had partially blocked the entrance to the compound. Gallagher's guys blew by them and the 10th Mountain's soldier could see, as Gallagher related,

"Some guy getting out of a smoking Humvee, with body parts and blood all over the place, I was missing a sleeve, I had a big compress on this side and I was just . . . yelling, Get the fuck out of the way! So they finally moved."

Now back on the airfield, Gallagher noted there

"was an Air Force Reserve aero medevac staging area, had nurses and doctors and totally not . . . that's where I took my organization, was straight there. . . . The people that were helping us get off the vehicles was the remainder of the people from our compound, so there were support people from the aviators, some of our cooks, some of the other special operators, that were in and around there. The Air Force Reservists were prepared for us to a degree, they weren't prepared for the type and amount of wounds that we had including Kowalewski with a live RPG sticking out of him."

Gallagher went on, "My men were started to be assisted out of the vehicles, we started the process of separating the dead from the wounded to triage them."

Although wounded, Gallagher also helped get his men out of the vehicles. The Command Sergeant Major of Delta came up to Gallagher and said,

"What are you doing?"

"I'm getting my men out of here," said Gallagher.

"You're pretty fucked up yourself. Let me take care of your men and let me get you some help."

The Sergeant Major then forced Gallagher out of the action and onto a stretcher.

Gallagher was medevaced to a U.N. hospital in Mogadishu on a UH-1H medical helicopter with a big red cross on it. Although drugged up, Gallagher remembers telling the crew chief,

"You gotta get guns on this helicopter!"

Gallagher later related "things they did that night saved my hand because they were going to amputate my hand." He went on, "Fighting is fighting, you got to do that anyway, but the real heroes are the people who took care of us afterwards."

Along with about 70 other wounded soldiers from Task Force

Ranger, Gallagher was flown to the U.S. Army hospital in Landstuhl, Germany. He remained there for twelve days, foregoing a trip to Walter Reed to keep the same doctor who performed four more operations on his hand. Gallagher was put in for a Silver Star for his actions in Mogadishu, but the award was downgraded to a Bronze Star with "V" device. Other awards for the operations ranged from the Medal of Honor to Army Commendation Medals.

Gallagher thought the bravest guys there were the machine gunners, all of whom were either killed or wounded, many after watching a fellow soldier shot out of the turret and then taking over their position until they too were hit.

Of his platoon, only one NCO, Aaron Weaver, was not killed or wounded. Weaver remained in the Army and later became warrant officer helicopter pilot. He later survived a bout with cancer but was killed in Iraq in a helicopter crash in December 2003. Sergeant Struecker, who drove PFC Blackburn back to the base, was later commissioned as an Army chaplain. He performed the services at Weaver's funeral in Florida, which Gallagher attended on January 17, 2004. Also at the Weaver's funeral were many of the rangers from Somalia, including Danny McKnight and Larry Moore.

Because of his wounds, Gallagher was released from the rangers and finally got a job with the Special Operations Command (SOCOM), where he worked closely with General Wayne Downing in air operations, doing a number of high altitude, low opening (HALO) jumps with him. Downing hand-selected Gallagher, because as he put it, Downing took care of "guys in my boat, you're hurt, no one wants to hire you because you're broken. The medical review board was chasing me down at Fort Benning to kick me out of the Army for my injuries."

While at SOCOM, Gallagher made E-8, Master Sergeant, and was reassigned to Hawaii for four years. During that time, he was the first sergeant of three different companies in the 25th Infantry Division. He was then picked up for E-9, Sergeant Major, and went to the Sergeants Major Academy at Fort Bliss, Texas. From there he was assigned to the 3rd Infantry Division at Fort Stewart, Georgia.

Gallagher took over as the Command Sergeant Major of the second brigade's 3rd Battalion, 15th Infantry regiment, a mechanized infantry unit in July 2002. The unit deployed to Kuwait in October 2002 for a routine rotation but became one of the lead infantry units in Iraqi Freedom.

Gallagher made the "ride up" in an M-88 tank recovery vehicle with NBC reporter David Bloom in tow as an embedded reporter. Now in his third war, Gallagher knew what to expect and where he would be needed. His assigned vehicle was a Humvee, but he quickly realized that a Humvee couldn't keep up with tanks. Instead he took over the battalion's huge tank recovery vehicle, the M-88, which could not only keep up with tanks and the mechanized infantry but also pull both out of ditches. The vehicle's imposing size gave a false sense of security and embedded reporters asked to ride along with Gallagher. They did not realize, however, that Gallagher was not going to hold back from the action, and the reporters quickly scrambled to find other rides after the ferocious battles in taking Baghdad.

Unfortunately, Bloom tragically died of a heart embolism on April 6, 2003, after riding in the vehicle since the start of the invasion.

On April 7, Gallagher played a key role in defending Objective Curly, one of three key road intersections leading into downtown Baghdad. He was also wounded again, this time in the leg. The intersections, much like an American interstate cloverleaf, were secured by Gallagher's battalion so that the brigade's tanks could safely ride through them on its "thunder runs" into downtown Baghdad. The thunder runs were to demonstrate to Saddam Hussein that the Americans were in his capitol and it was time to surrender. Because there were three intersections, the battalion operations officer named them *Larry, Curly* and *Moe* after the Three Stooges and assigned a rifle platoon to each intersection.

Gallagher's actions at Objective Curly are best summed up by him taking a quick break during an hours-long firefight to make a cup of coffee, receiving double takes from soldiers deep in a pitched battle seeing their sergeant major calmly drinking a cup of joe. During the din of battle, he harassed the medics for not bringing rifles with them and vainly shooting back at attackers with pistols. Gallagher sharply reminded them that while back at Fort Stewart, they rejected his pleas to spend more time on rifle marksmanship.

His actions at Curly were photographed by embedded reporters, and one picture wound up on the cover of *Army* magazine and in the *Wall Street Journal*. He was subsequently awarded the Silver Star for his actions in Iraq. The 2004 Veteran's Day issue of the *Wall Street Journal* had a photograph of Gallagher standing next to his M-88, shooting back at Iraqi attackers while an Army captain was bandaging up his wounded leg. It is pure Gallagher.

Gallagher ended his career at Fort Belvoir, Virginia, in 2013 as the senior enlisted leader of the U.S. Army Wounded Warrior Program, a unit for wounded soldiers. No one was more suited for that job.

In a harsher world, Gallagher should have died at birth. Surviving that and many missteps, he never should have been allowed to enlist in the Army. And even then, serving in the Army's elite units should have been out of his reach. But he did. Heroes come from all places and circumstances but few have overcome so much as Black Hawk Bob. He will be missed.

Bob Johnson retired from the Army Reserve as an infantry major in 1995. He volunteered for recall in 2007 and served in Afghanistan as an infantry operations officer of the Panjshir Provincial Reconstruction Team in northeast Afghanistan in 2008. He has a B.A. in English from Virginia Military Institute and an M.A. in writing from Johns Hopkins University. Bob has had two non-fiction books published and recently finished his first novel, *Team Lion*. He was awarded a Bronze Star Medal for his service in Afghanistan.